214 photographs by
Edwin Smith

English Parish Churches

INTRODUCTORY TEXTS BY
GRAHAM HUTTON

NOTES ON THE PLATES BY
OLIVE COOK

Thames and Hudson · London

To the memory of
Edwin Smith
1912 – 1971
an admirable artist and a lover of England's parish churches

On the half-title page: a bell-ringing angel in the south aisle roof of St John the Baptist, Stamford, Lincolnshire.

On the title page: St Mary, Whitby, in the North Riding of Yorkshire (see p. 177 and pl. 170).

Introductory texts © 1976 Hutton Economic Services
Text and photographs by Edwin Smith and notes on the plates © 1976 Olive Cook

Printed in Great Britain by Jarrold and Sons Ltd, Norwich

Contents

On photographing cathedrals and parish churches * by Edwin Smith

I arrive looking as much as possible like any other visitor, equipment discreetly satchelled and not draped around my person. Taking the first opportunity I dump bag and tripod beneath a bench, behind a pier or on any obscure stone ledge or underneath the collecting box table. A cathedral is rather like a railway station in its number and variety of crannies of this kind (though very unlike of course in the confidence it encourages that what is left will remain against one's return). An image arises of this bag as the last deposit on a ghostly pile of travellers' bundles that have been left in such crannies over a minimum of 500 years, and with it the realization that one's mind is starting to digest the atmosphere. It is probably 9 a.m., and the verger may be ringing the bell for Matins; soon a tiny file of clergy will advance from the vestry off the south choir aisle and, making two slow right-angled turns, pass into the choir. I am conscious of a certain reluctance at not supporting them, but I have come to worship with the eye and to give other kinds of praise. As I tread softly in another direction the thin monotone of devotion heightens my reactions to the vistas around me.

If I am lucky the morning is clear but not sunny, or if there is sun it is weak or frequently screened by cloud. For in this preliminary stroll I am rehearsing for the camera and thinking of its peculiar needs rather than of the immediate pleasure of the more adaptable eye. Brilliance and great contrast, delicious to the eye, are disastrous to the photographic process, and I am seeking the vantage points that not only compose in terms of form but where the range of light and shade falls within the scope of the film. Every photographer favours a particular direction of light: I am drawn to situations where the source of light lies diagonally in front of me and not behind. To this direction I react instinctively and I gravitate without conscious design to those parts of the structure where this light obtains. These parts of the building I sense are 'working' for me, but they will of course rapidly be replaced by others as the light moves round.

So, having received the suggestion of a number of possibilities that make me excited to begin, I retrace my steps. By now Matins will be over, the sparse file of devout will have returned to the vestry, the verger, having removed his surplice, will be found in black habit not far from one of the great piers of the crossing. Explaining my purpose to him – signing his book, paying a fee, producing a letter of permission from the Dean and Chapter, whatever the circumstances demand – I get permission to begin.

I work quickly, discreetly and always in the lighting conditions that exist at the moment, the camera, with a focusing screen that necessitates the use of a black

6

cloth over the head, always on a tripod, and with exposures that vary in duration from about ten seconds to as many minutes. With luck it will still be early enough for the cathedral to be relatively deserted and I try to get through with general views while there is still no more than an occasional visitor to avoid. Long exposures have the advantage that they can be divided, the lens being covered while anyone saunters across its path, and I have sometimes divided a minute's exposure into as many as thirty separate units as absorbed visitors pass in and out of sight behind piers and monuments. My favourite visitors sit in bemused tranquillity, showing no movement during an exposure of several minutes, or are dressed darkly and move briskly which means they leave no trace. Very wearing are pairs of ladies in white who take ten minutes to stroll down a 200-foot aisle engaged in eager conversation, or become engrossed in the irrelevant details of a modern monument half-way down.

The visitor population of cathedrals varies seasonally and geographically. Always less in winter and always less in the north and east than in the south and west. Ely Cathedral on a midwinter afternoon with no more than a single local fugitive from the freezing fenland huddled round one of its giant stoves is desolate and heart-piercing. Canterbury any time between early spring and late autumn can be as busy as the concourse of a railway terminal and as bitterly bewildering.

The great cathedral is a public experience. Not with the greatest good fortune could one hope to enjoy it quite alone, nor perhaps would it be comfortable to do so. But the parish church, outside the hours of conventional worship, is for private experience and it is the rarest misfortune to share it with anyone less effacing, less part of the ambience, than the practising organist, the altar flower arranger or a very occasional incumbent.

For me, photography in a good village church is unalloyed bliss. A cathedral is a great machine, impressive and mysterious, and one can rarely visit it without making a special effort. However tranquilly isolated in its own close it eventually proves to be, one has to brave the traffic of its town, the confusion of its streets and the mundane irritations of its parking arrangements.

But it is possible to come upon the perfect village church quite by chance, breaking a journey on impulse, entering without premeditation to receive some of the most exquisite pleasure that building can offer. The visual pleasures and surprises of visiting country churches have been among the most vivid and poignant of my life, and it is a perpetual source of wonder and gratitude to me that it is possible to walk casually into these marvellously articulated structures, to be surprised, delighted, diverted, amused and deeply moved without being disturbed by the presence of a single other person. At all hours of the day, long after I was expected elsewhere or have found a hotel for the night, I have hurried back to the car for my equipment and begun working – entranced by the sense of communion with something admired to intensity, intoxicated by the privilege of being able to pay it the homage of my craft. I must confess that I seldom risk breaking this spell by actually asking permission, for speech dilutes vision; and I offer apologies to the incumbents of many churches for this discourtesy.

Foreword

Twenty-four years ago, after three years' collaboration between two friends, respectively author and photographer, Thames and Hudson published *English Parish Churches* (Hutton and Smith, 1952). It was the first substantial study of its subject after the war of 1939–45 and coincided with the setting up of the Historic Churches Preservation Trust, which made use of Edwin Smith's remarkable plates in exhibitions throughout the country. It started a kind of chain reaction of public interest in, and excellent books about, England's parish churches. Both that interest and those books continue to flourish; but our original work has for many years been unobtainable save in libraries.

Edwin died in 1971 leaving upwards of 2,000 of his inimitable plates of English churches and their contents – his loving and abiding interest – nearly all taken in the twenty years after 1952. Our publishers accordingly suggested to his widow, Olive Cook, and to me that we might draw on those mainly unpublished studies to make a new selection of plates and furnish with it a longer explanatory text than had been feasible in 1952, particularly for the wider and more mobile public interested in such churches which had come into being after Edwin's and my original book.

That is the origin of this work and of its dedication. All involved in its preparation – and more people, and their talents, and their devoted collaboration are in fact so involved than most readers imagine – hope it will help readers to share some of Edwin's interest in, and love for, England's parish churches. Despite amalgamations of parishes and of 'cures' for souls, and despite diminishing numbers of the priesthood and their flocks, more lay folk seem interested in and concerned about these churches than they did to us a quarter of a century ago. Possibly it is not 'despite' such things but 'because of' them. English parish churches are increasingly, acceleratingly more menaced with extinction than then. At the present rate of extinction of historic parish churches solely in rural areas (not in towns and cities), by the year 2000 England will have lost one out of every six at present remaining: a grievous destruction of what by common consent of all authorities constitutes the nation's greatest collective heritage of art, architecture and craftsmanship. Indeed, broadly one-quarter of all existing parish churches in England are now threatened with demolition or conversion out of all recognition.

Happily the Redundant Churches Fund set up in 1968 by Church and State is not – yet – being called on to conserve *historic* parish churches (roughly half the total) at so pitiable a rate, though in the last two years the rate has alarmingly accelerated. Happily, too, the Historic Churches Preservation Trust, and many voluntary bodies staffed by lay folk of goodwill (like the Friends of Friendless Churches and many little local parish or inter-parish conservation societies) aided by priests, are indefatigable in organizing and financing the preservation of many historic churches which in default of such devotion would by now have become nameless, placeless, lost without trace. Not the most zealous atheist, nor the most modernist of priests, could justify the loss of one-half of all our parish churches by the 1980s as an enlargement of the human spirit, or of human beings' lives, or even only of aesthetic experience (only!). The warning of such a rate of loss through declared 'redundancy' was issued by the Bridges Commission in 1960.

A few words of explanation about this book are due. First, we have deemed it wise to retain the old English county boundaries (not the new, strange, and still largely unknown urban, con-urban, and other local governmental monstrosities) because all guide, architectural, and topographical reference books refer to the old county lines: e.g. Sir Nikolaus Pevsner's famous *Buildings of England* series. The new locations, where they apply, will be found in the index. Secondly, however the churches of parishes began – some as cathedrals, others abbeys, minsters, priories and so on – we have kept to parish churches as they now are (or, alas! have till recently been); if a former parish church has become a cathedral, the reader is referred to Mr Alec Clifton-Taylor's companion volume in this series, *The Cathedrals of England*. Edwin Smith's diagram of typical ground-plans from our original work has been used again here (p. 243), but I have re-compiled the select bibliography (p. 246). Finally, the conventional orientation of chancels is assumed and portions of a church thus defined (the chancel at the east, the 'right-hand aisle' the south aisle, and so on).

Though the selection and descriptive captions of the plates are Olive Cook's work, and the text (and appendices) mine, a work like this does not see the light without much mutual discussion, suggestion and help. So it is only right to express gratitude here for the patient assistance of our publishers and of my wife, Marjorie Hutton.

London, March 1976   G.H.

CHAPTER ONE

Before the Conquest

THE ENGLISH PARISH and its church came into being in the period between the first settlements by Angles, Saxons, Jutes and Frisians in the low-lying lands of eastern and south-eastern England in the fifth century, and the emergence of the far different, far more 'English' England after the wars between the Anglo-Saxons and the Danish-Norse invaders and settlers in the eastern half of England five centuries later. Indeed the pattern of English parishes and their churches recorded in Domesday Book, compiled twenty years after the Norman Conquest in 1066, remained almost unvaried until the Industrial Revolution began to expand the number and size of towns and cities in the latter half of the eighteenth century. The rural, overwhelmingly agricultural, and only partly commercial England lasted a millennium, roughly from 850 to 1850; modern, overwhelmingly urban England is but the outcome of the last 100 years. These two 'Englands' co-exist and overlap today as parishes in cities, towns and suburbs meet the bounds of surrounding country parishes. But before there were parishes Britain had churches.

There was quite a flourishing Christian Church in Roman Britain during the last century of Roman rule. Tertullian, the great apologist for Christianity writing about the year 200, boasted that the Church had 'subdued territories of the Britons not yet reached by Romans', which may mean the Celtic, non-Roman-settled parts of Britain (in what we now call Wales and Scotland, or even perhaps Ireland), but which almost certainly means localities 'beyond the pale' of the Roman settlement and administration in the upper and lower 'Britains' into which the province was divided. So from about 200 to just on 600, when St Augustine landed in Kent, there were four centuries of Church life, Romano-British or (later) Celtic, in what was to become 'England': a Church falling back to the western and northern periphery of the country as the heathen, illiterate Anglo-Saxons and Jutes made their way up the eastern and southern river valleys, settling the lower-lying (hitherto largely unsettled) heavier clayish lands, clearing the 'forest primeval'; living and toiling rough, and fighting more roughly, for direly needed land; banded together in kinship and followership which gave (from the Anglo-Saxon genitive of some leader's name) those innumerable eastern and southern village names ending in '-ing', '-ings', or somewhat later '-ingham' or '-ington' – like Hastings, Lastingham, Rustington.

The 'England' which confronted Augustine in about 600 was a land of sharp, bitter divisions: above all between the heathen Anglo-Saxon or Jutish kingdoms of the Heptarchy (in what was becoming England proper) and the nominally (and sometimes devotedly) Christian Celtic kingdoms to the north and west. But hardly less bitter were the divisions within and between all of these kingdoms, Christian or not, Celtic or Anglo-Saxon. The old Roman towns went under,

11

1 All Saints, Brixworth, Northamptonshire

mistrusted by the invading settlers; most of the big Romano-British estates (the *villae*) were broken up; land went back to grass or was swamped, as in the Fens.

Yet in this chaos of warring petty states the Church was at work on both sides; and this 'dark age' of the English nation is important here because, as it unfolded, English parishes and their churches took their shapes. These shapes are distinctive for a reason not found on the continent of Europe.

The Teutonic tribes who irrupted overland into the Western Roman Empire adopted in a short time the religion, fashions, speech and civil administration of the Romanized indigenous peoples. Not so the Angles, Saxons, Jutes and Frisians who came across the North Sea and Channel to what was to become England. They pushed the indigenous Celts west and north, and Celtic Christianity with them: the Celtic Church was thus almost insulated from Rome. As the invaders laid the foundations of a new 'England' east of the line from Berwick on Tweed to Exmouth, based on new villages and agriculture, they preserved their language and heathen gods for the two dark centuries between the going of the Romans and the coming of Augustine's mission. They intermarried so little with the indigenous Romano-British Celts that the old Celtic tongue survived nowhere in their English lands except in a few place and personal names. Indeed, the various Celtic kingdoms and their folk steadfastly refused to have any persistent and peaceable intercourse with the Teutonic intruders into Britain.

So insulated from the Continent and the changes in the Roman rites and practices had the Celtic Church become by the time Augustine and his fellow-missionaries began their work in 597 that it rejected his overtures for an accommodation of Christian doctrines and rites. Thus there arose two distinctive and rival streams of Christian thought and teaching in England: that of the Roman Church of Gregory and Augustine in the south and east, and that of the old Celtic Church in the north and west and in Ireland. From Ireland Columba and Ninian carried Christianity to Western Scotland, and from Scotland the mission of Aidan went out early in the seventh century to re-convert lapsed Northumbria and to evangelize Mercia.

Irish Christianity was monastic and tribal, and the Irish monastery acknowledged no ecclesiastical authority superior to its abbot. It thus could never become the basis for a parochial system and was not, in the Roman sense, administered by bishops. Celtic monasticism moreover differed sharply from the ideals and practices of St Benedict. The Irish monastery was a congregation of hermits in some remote spot, each living in his own beehive hut. There were other trivial differences – the Celts had a date for Easter which differed from that of Rome, and their priest-monks shaved their heads from ear to ear across the front of the head instead of adopting the round tonsure on the crown. But the important differences of spirit and organization were of course those which sprang from the question of submission to Rome.

The two streams of thought met for a final confrontation at the famous Synod of Whitby, summoned in 664 by Oswy, King of Northumbria, soon after – under the influence of his wife and of Paulinus, who had been sent to England by Gregory in 601 and had been consecrated a bishop at Canterbury – he had rejected the Celtic

Church of Iona in favour of that of Rome. Upon the resolution of the Synod to follow the teaching and rites of Rome, the old Celtic Church and its missions retired from the English kingdoms.

The ancient disparities between the forms of Christian teaching had a lasting effect on the physical aspect of the English parish church, just as the division between the Celtic peoples of Britain, who lived mainly in the highlands, and the overwhelmingly Teutonic and Scandinavian village-makers and forest-clearers of the lowlands, is expressed in the shapes of fields, in the choice of wood or stone for building, in place and family names and above all in customs and beliefs. In one particular the old-fashioned, overcome Celtic Church, withdrawing from England, achieved a notable and paradoxical victory, a victory which is visible everywhere in the rectangular eastern ends of English parish churches. On the Continent chancels generally to this day end in a semicircle or apse, and this plan, based on the Roman basilica, was the one reintroduced into Kent by Augustine and his followers. But the English obstinately preferred the square-ended chancel. This, together with the east window, may perpetuate a pagan tradition which demanded that altar and celebrant should be bathed in the full light of the morning sun. For thirteen centuries this has constituted the dominant feature of the distinctive English style. But that is not how it began: and to 'how it began' we must now turn.

The Celtic church plan was closely allied to the earliest form of church of which we know anything decisive, the simple, tall narrow cell of the catacombs, generally barrel-vaulted and with a little holy place or sanctuary beyond what we would now call its nave, in which the priest officiated. In its most primitive form the Irish oratory consisted of a rectangular cell of wood or stone like the famous Gallerus Oratory near Dingle. In time a small rectangular chamber or sanctuary reserved for the altar was built at one end. This basic plan is preserved in the remains of a sanctuary at Madron, near Land's End in Cornwall, and it was the plan of the church of St Martin at Canterbury, which Bede says was built while the Romans were still in the island and used as an oratory by Bertha, the Christian wife of pagan Ethelbert of Kent.

The Roman basilican church plan was modelled on that of the pagan administrative hall and law-court, with two rows of columns along what we now call the nave (from the Latin *navis*, ship, probably because of its shape and also because of the symbolism of the 'ship of salvation'), aisles on either side, with roofs sloping towards the upper nave walls in which appeared a row of windows (the clerestory), a vestibule at one end and an apse at the other end. Projecting from each side of the building at the junction of the apse and the nave there might be a square chamber known as the *porticus*, later to develop into the transept. When first incorporated into Christian church plans, the porticus served as a sacristy or chapel, as at Bradwell juxta Mare, Essex, where the plan has been revealed by excavation although the two porticus no longer exist.

The adoption of the basilican plan was probably influenced by the Emperor Constantine's gift in 312 of the basilica in his palace of the Lateran for use as the cathedral church of Rome. The earliest churches of Augustine's mission were

constructed on this Roman plan. Except for Bradwell juxta Mare, they were all in Kent and were built of stone by craftsmen brought by the mission from Italy or Gaul. They included St Andrew, Rochester (604), St Mary and St Pancras, Canterbury (both *c.* 620), St Mary, Lyminge (*c.* 637) and St Mary, Reculver (669,
1 demolished 1805). Their plan was followed in the noble basilica of Brixworth,
p. 243 Northamptonshire (*c.* 680), at Worth, Sussex (early tenth century) and at Wing,
6 Buckinghamshire (tenth century). Wing is the most complete example of the plan, for not only do the porticus survive, almost taking on the importance of transepts, but there are aisles, and aisles are rare in surviving Anglo-Saxon churches. Brixworth had aisles divided from the nave by arcades of round arches springing from heavy rectangular piers instead of the columns of the Roman basilica. But excavations have shown that the aisles were blocked transversely, from north to south, at an early date to form a series of porticus or separate chambers.

A few of these basilican churches followed the Italian custom of building the sanctuary over a small undercroft which might contain the relics or body of a saint.
4 Saxon crypts remain at Hexham, Repton, Ripon and Wing. At Brixworth the apse was surrounded by an *external* ring-crypt, a sunk, tunnel-vaulted passage, a feature first found at St Peter's, Rome (*c.* 590).

The first churches of the Northumbrian school followed the 'Celtic' plan of an aisleless, box-like nave leading into a narrower, square-ended chancel. Bede's testimony shows that these churches were generally built of wood. He says, for instance, that Edwin, King of Northumbria, was baptised by Paulinus at York on Easter Day 627 in the church of St Peter, which he had built of timber, and that the church at Lindisfarne was built *more Scottorum* (after the manner of the Irish) 'not of stone, but entirely of sawn oak'. Wooden structures, whether they consisted of timber framing filled with wattle and daub or of split trunks of trees (like the surviving nave of Greenstead, Essex), did not readily lend themselves to semicircular forms, and this was presumably one reason for the persistence (in abundantly forested Anglo-Saxon England) of the rectangular chancel. In a church
2 such as Monkwearmouth, for the building of which Benedict Biscop brought masons from Gaul, the Roman style of stone building was combined with a
p.243 square-ended sanctuary, as it was at Jarrow, Corbridge, Escomb and Repton.

We do not really know how the English parish originated. The word comes from the pagan Roman Empire where it meant a big region like a province. In the early Church it meant, at one time, a collection of believers of the same racial or regional origin in the same city, so that one could talk of the 'parish' of the Gauls, or the Spaniards, or the Tunisians, in Rome itself. When first used in the Church in England it meant the territory of a bishop – what we now call a diocese, which is also a term taken from the pagan Roman Empire. The first churches were 'cathedrals', i.e. 'seats' of missionary bishops.

As villages were formed, homesteads established, 'hundreds' and 'tithings' of neighbours organized in little localities, cultivating their fields in common, serving a local thegn or lord, and as the Church advanced its missionary work, the first little wooden churches were built, belonging to the local lord who built them. He could even dismantle them, remove them, or turn them into mills or other secular buildings. He claimed the right of appointing the parish priest, a right which remained with the lord of the manor throughout the Middle Ages and in some cases still continues. The nearness of the manor house to the church in so many villages bears witness to the close relationship. Thus the first parish priests were the chaplains of Saxon thegns; they were not monks and in Saxon times, and even after, they were often married. The priest's duty required him to celebrate seven services daily. After the eleventh century three daily services were deemed sufficient in parish churches.

The lord's manor – itself at times the holding of a monastery of collegiate foundation – was the ultimate territorial unit under the Anglo-Saxons, as well as the ultimate legal and administrative unit. Where the population was sparse, as in the uplands of the north and centre, one parish would contain, and still does, more than one village, more than one lord's manor or holding. On the other hand, when an original settlement or village or manor was very large or became a township – and later a city – it was split into many parishes. By the year 1000 the parishes and their churches were distributed mainly as they appear in rural England today. It is remarkable how many Saxon parish boundaries have survived through centuries of change. A walk along a parish boundary can still reveal the outline, sometimes even the natural features of an Anglo-Saxon estate.

The financial basis of the parish was a system of 'tithes', or offerings to the church of a tenth part of the annual produce of the parish lands either in money or in kind, a system which became open to abuse and was the subject of litigation throughout the early Middle Ages. Originally a fourth part of the tithes was devoted to the upkeep of the church fabric. After the Conquest, when the appropriation of churches to the monastic and collegiate establishments became common, it was usual for the rector, or administrator of the tithes, to maintain only the chancel from these funds: maintenance of the nave, often a heavy burden, became the responsibility of the parishioners.

From the beginning of the Anglo-Saxon period until the end of the twelfth century the Church may well have absorbed one-half of the economic resources and manpower of England, not only in buildings, with all their accompaniments of stone and wood carving, carpentry, painting, glazing, tile-making, plasterwork, thatching and leadwork, but in education (for the Church ran the only schools and the most promising boys were engaged in its service), the training of administrators and the encouragement of agricultural techniques. A cleric was always literate, but an earl was not necessarily so until the reforms of Alfred and Athelstan brought the gifts of learning to the sons of thegns and noblemen.

Few people today pause to consider the words for 'church' in our various languages. In the Teutonic tongues, English, German and Dutch, the word for the Christian assembly-hall is *church*, *Kirche*, *Kerk*, from the original Celtic *ciric*, pronounced *chirich*, which originally meant only the 'holy ground', or church-*yard*, or place of Christian burial. What we now call a church was not so called until as late as the tenth century.

From the time of Augustine's coming until 1066 three main kinds of churches arose: (1) the early diocesan cathedrals, whose dioceses were modified over the years by wars or civil readjustments; (2) the monastic and collegiate churches, harbouring monks or priests dedicated to God's work, but also undertaking the clearing of forests and agriculture as ever more lands were allotted or bequeathed to them; and (3) the churches built by secular lords for their dependents. These last are the prototypes of the English parish church. While the cathedrals and the monastic and collegiate churches were designed to meet the doctrinal needs of the clergy, the parish church was built to serve a village, hamlet or collection of such settlements where the same folk lived, worked and died. The parish church and the graveyard in which it was set were the centre of village life, both mundane and spiritual. They were associated with the deepest of human feelings, joy and sorrow as well as the pleasures of festivals and saints' days, especially the annual feast known as the Church Ale. This was held in the nave and was followed by dancing. It was started by Pope Gregory VII to take the place of the sacrifice of cattle and horses, accompanied by feasting and dancing, which was common in pagan Britain.

Public notices still posted in church porches remind us that the porch was the usual place for the transaction of much of the civil business of the parish from the earliest times; for deliberations and discussions on communal legal and economic matters, especially those connected with agriculture and questions of tenure. Here the marriage service might be held, here parts of the rites of Baptism were celebrated, and here those who broke their vows did penance in a white sheet.

Church and churchyard also provided security. The churchyard was a refuge to which in troubled times men took their few chattels and drove their stock. This use of the churchyard appears in the first surviving roll of pleas of the Crown for Yorkshire, and though it dates from just after the Conquest it refers to established custom. A man accused of maiming his enemy pleads that his accuser lost his hand in true judgment for stealing a cow from a churchyard where it should have been inviolate.

The walls of the church were plastered over within and often, if it was small, without. Walls, mouldings and statuary were gilded and decorated, chiefly in distemper in earth colours (red and yellow ochre, charcoal black, lime white and terre verte) with designs varying from simple diapers to complicated compositions. Bede, writing of St Wilfrid's church at Hexham, says it was adorned with 'pictures and colours of great and wonderful variety'. They must have resembled the later decorative schemes which can be seen at Pickering in Yorkshire, Copford in Essex, Baunton in Gloucestershire, and Chaldon in Surrey; for the choice of subject had been determined on principles laid down by the Church at the Second Council of Nicaea in 787. The commonest themes were the Last Judgment and St Christopher with the Child, though the walls might be covered with a series of pictures showing the Life and Passion of Christ or the Life of the Virgin, or with paintings of the apostles, as at Kempley, Gloucestershire, where the work is carried out in true fresco (pigments applied to a freshly laid coat of wet plaster before it has had time to absorb carbonic acid from the air). It is hard today to imagine the splendid effect of the parish church and its contents amid the poor hovels of the early villages, especially on men and women wresting a bare living from the fields, isolated from other settlements and with only one place of resort apart from their homes.

Up to 1066 the total population of Britain, including Wales and what came to be called Scotland, did not exceed 2 million souls. During that Anglo-Saxon period building in stone, as we have seen, was rare, and bricks were not made. Transport and quarrying presented almost insurmountable difficulties, for there existed only the old Roman arterial roads and machinery was primitive. So exceptional was a church of stone in earlier Saxon times that St Ninian's church at Whithorn in Galloway, built of that material, was, according to Bede, popularly known as 'Candida Casa' – the white house. The very word for 'to build' in Old English, *timbrian*, implies a timbered structure. Bede testifies to the high quality of the workmanship of Saxon wood-built churches, most of which were destroyed by fire or, together with most of the stone-built churches, wholly or partly replaced by new buildings after the Conquest. Nevertheless in England as a whole as many as 250 Saxon or part-Saxon parish churches survive.

With the squared east end (p. 13) goes the English preference for an entrance by a *p. 243* side porch, generally on the south (pp. 38–39), rather than at the west as on the Continent. The Saxon south porch at Bishopstone in Sussex and the remains of a south porch at Bradford on Avon in Wiltshire testify to the establishment of this preference in pre-Conquest England. But some Saxon churches exhibit west tower doors or western porches, as in the lower storeys of the towers at Monkwearmouth *1, 2* and Brixworth, and in eleventh-century buildings entrance by a west door was not uncommon.

The addition of stone towers to the simple Saxon plan was probably a result of the Danish invasions: they occur near the coasts of Northumberland, Durham, Lincolnshire and East Anglia. The stone tower seems often to have replaced a former timber structure, and served not only to house the bells but as a landmark, a look-out and perhaps occasionally a refuge. Sometimes, as at Brixworth and Deerhurst, there is a room in an upper stage of the tower with a window which *7, 8* looks down into the nave: perhaps the parish priest was housed there, but neither this nor the use of such a window is yet certain.

The commonest position for the tower was at the west end, and this is again typically English. Some towers were raised above the western porch of an earlier Saxon church, as at Brixworth and Monkwearmouth. The cruciform plan with a central tower over the crossing was rare before the Conquest, though it exists in the late Saxon church of Breamore (where, however, the transepts are mere porticus, *10* much lower than the nave), and a tower was clearly intended over the true crossing of Stow, Lincolnshire. *9*

The importance of Saxon parish churches is great, because in them alone can we see the Saxon architectural style. No cathedral remains, apart from the amorphous ruins of North Elmham in Norfolk. Each Saxon church makes its own contribution to our knowledge of a long period of high aesthetic achievement – whether it be the stark, startling exterior and monumental, Italianate interior of Brixworth, the delicately ornamented towers of Earls Barton, Barton on Humber, *12, 13*

14   Sompting and Stanton Lacy, the touchingly simple interior of two-celled Escomb;
11   or the bold, ambitious composition of Worth; or Wing, with its raised chancel and
6   polygonal arcaded apse. Saxon work is so strikingly distinctive that the merest
       fragment of architecture or sculpture is instantly recognizable. The Seated Christ at
15, 16 Barnack, the Madonna and Child of Inglesham, the two Crucifixions at Langford,
       and the large blessing angel at Breedon-on-the-Hill, to mention but a few of the
       surviving Saxon architectural sculptures, are animated by a sense of humanity, and
       show a sensitivity and a softness of modelling beside which the first efforts of the
       Norman sculptors, however vital, look violent and crude.

       Even in the Saxon period the strong sense of locality is evident which gives
       medieval parish church architecture such variety. While the builders of the great
       abbey churches and cathedrals were independent of local conditions, parish church
       builders had to rely on the materials immediately available. The advantages of a
       site on the broad band of oolitic limestone, which stretches diagonally across
       England from Somerset through Gloucestershire, Wiltshire, Oxfordshire,
       Northamptonshire and Lincolnshire, show up already in the stonework of
       Bradford on Avon, Barnack, Earls Barton, Brixworth, Geddington, Stow, and
       Wittering, where the powerful chancel arch is among the most arresting of all
       parish church features. In East Anglia and parts of Berkshire and Sussex, regions of
       chalk and flint, Roman materials were sometimes re-used as at Bradwell juxta
       Mare; or the building was of flint and rubble like the tower of St Bene't's,
       Cambridge, with quoins of imported stone; or the use of stone was avoided by
21   building round flint towers, as at Haddiscoe in Norfolk. The poignant, archaic
2, 3, 5 atmosphere of churches like those at Monkwearmouth, Escomb and Bradford on
       Avon arises largely from the contrast between their small proportions and the
       great stones used in their fabric.

       Disproportionate space may be thought to have been devoted to the six
       centuries of Anglo-Saxon and Danish rule, and to the half-millennium of the
       Church in England. But when Duke William of Normandy was crowned William
       I of England the country was already a settled, organized, going concern. Its early
       nucleated villages and later separate homesteads had been given churches and
       parishes: greater or lesser churches; one-village or many-village parishes. The
       entire (though still narrow) extent of cultivable land was covered by Church and
       State authorities for ecclesiastical, civil and military purposes. The population was
       small; but the Anglo-Saxon improvements in agriculture had well-nigh banished
       famine; and the standards of arts and craftsmanship were rated as high as any on the
       Continent – witness such disparate arts and crafts as calligraphy, illumination,
       sculpture, fine ivory and wood carving, church-building, painting and
       embroidery. The status of women was higher than it was elsewhere in Europe and
       higher than it ever was again in England before the present century. The people
       were famed throughout Europe for devoutness; the (by now reformed) priesthood,
       for devotion. This was the England described by William's assessors in Domesday
       Book, on the basis of which his barons and prelates proceeded to raze the Saxon
       churches and build them anew, together with many new churches, in bigger and
       bolder dimensions and in a new style.

Notes on the plates

1 All Saints, Brixworth, Northamptonshire: view from the south
The church dates from the remote period (about 675) when the kingdom of Mercia had but just become Christian, and while its rugged form nobly testifies to the new faith it still evokes Roman colonial traditions. The thin bricks, arranged in double rows for strength round the arches, red against the dark ironstone rubble of the fabric, are Roman and the arches themselves are part of a Roman basilican plan which links All Saints to Augustine's group of Roman-inspired churches in Kent, for they originally divided the nave from now-vanished aisles. The base of the present tower was at first a two-storeyed porch. The tower was raised above it and the projecting stair turret added some time after 870, when the Danes destroyed the monastery to which Brixworth was attached. It was then that All Saints became a parish church.

2 St Peter with St Cuthbert, Monkwearmouth, Co. Durham: west front
The vitality of this lean, archaic tower (only eleven feet square and sixty feet high), and tall, thin nave built of rubble and irregular cut stones is enhanced by its contrast with the smooth-faced Victorian aisle. Bede (who spent all his adult life at Jarrow, Monkwearmouth's sister-monastery) tells us that St Peter's was built 'on the Roman model', but he is referring only to the use of stone: the plan is that of a Celtic church, with an aisleless nave and square-ended chancel. It was founded in 674 by Benedict Biscop, a remarkable Northumbrian noble-man who became a monk in southern France and then served as abbot of St Peter and St Paul at Canterbury. He visited Rome six times and brought back pictures, manuscripts and foreign craftsmen to enrich his Northumbrian foundations, Monkwearmouth and Jarrow. Through him

John, the arch-chanter of St Peter's in Rome, introduced the art of Gregorian chant to England, where it was sung for the first time in this little church.

As at Brixworth, the upper stages of the tower were added to a western porch, probably in the tenth century. The tower shows two characteristic Saxon windows: the round-arched opening cut from a single stone and the twin-arched bell window with a short dividing shaft of baluster form. The enclosing arch of thin stone slabs, more like an outline than a solid form, is another typically Saxon convention. Circular openings like the one seen here occasionally occur in Saxon belfries, as much as effective accents in the design as for their use as additional sound-holes. Above the lower window are the defaced remains of a giant image, the first representation of the human figure on a British church. Monkwearmouth became parochial at the Dissolution.

3 St Lawrence, Bradford on Avon, Wiltshire: view across the nave from the north porticus
The tall, narrow proportions characteristic of Saxon churches are experienced with peculiar intensity in this tiny interior because the church has never been enlarged since the beginning of the eighth century. The stilted arch, the crude capitals and roll-mouldings of the tall opening, scarcely three feet wide, into the nave, the large, finely jointed stones of the nave wall, all remain as they were when this 'churchlet' of a monastery, founded according to William of Malmesbury by St Aldhelm, was completed. Originally there was another porticus opposite the one from which we are looking. (See also p. 13 and pl. 5.)

4 St Wystan, Repton, Derbyshire: crypt
The crypt is among the few in England which were actually used as the final resting place of the saint to whom the church is

dedicated. It was originally built in the seventh century to serve as a mausoleum for the royal house of Mercia. Wystan, son of Wimund and heir to the Mercian throne, was buried here after he had been treacherously killed in June 850 by his godfather, enraged by Wystan's opposition to his marriage to Wimund's widow. Scarcely the death of a martyr. Yet miracles followed the murder and Wystan was canonized. The two passages which still connect the crypt with the church above were made at this time for the use of pilgrims who flocked to the shrine. Destroyed by the Danes, the crypt was rebuilt as part of a new church towards the close of the tenth century, the date of the columns and vaulted roof. Eventually it was sealed and forgotten, not to be rediscovered until 1779, when a grave was being dug in the chancel above it for Dr Prior, headmaster of Repton School.

5 St Lawrence, Bradford on Avon, Wiltshire: chancel
6 All Saints, Wing, Buckinghamshire: apse
The two chancels not only present a lively contrast in texture between chalk and flint rubble and regularly coursed ashlar (a rarity in Saxon buildings), but eloquently illustrate the difference in type between the apsidal plan reintroduced into England by St Augustine and the square-ended Celtic plan which in Wessex, where both Glastonbury and Malmesbury were Celtic foundations, had long been dominant. The shallow wall arcading with which both buildings are adorned suggests a tenth-century date and may have been inspired by examples in Ottonian Germany or in northern Italy. Certainly the shape of the Wing apse evokes, most movingly if falteringly, the apses of the Early Christian churches at Ravenna. St Lawrence (see also pl. 3) was founded before St Aldhelm's death in 709, and Wing has been shown to have been also an eighth-century foundation. In both cases the ornament was added later. At Wing it was applied, at Bradford on Avon it was – astonishingly – cut out of the masonry.

7 St Mary, Deerhurst, Gloucestershire: window in the west wall of the nave
These triangular-headed openings, which

are as characteristic of Saxon architecture as the round arch and baluster shaft, are, like the similarly sited window at Brixworth (pl. 7), features of a tower added to an existing porch about 900. They must have served a similar purpose. Fashioned of pale oolitic limestone, this poetic union of massive triangular, hooded heads (faint echoes of pediments), queer stepped capitals (echoes of entablatures), classically fluted jambs and a fluted, square-cut central pier instead of the customary baluster, surprises and delights the eye in the same way as the unlikely association of Gothic and classic in Elizabethan architecture.

8 All Saints, Brixworth, Northamptonshire: west wall of the nave
Here again we see Roman materials re-used (compare pl. 1). The lowest arch leads into the tower, originally a porch. The blocked arch above, with part of its brick head showing through the plaster, may perhaps have led from the upper storey of the porch into a gallery. The upper threefold opening displays the baluster shafts of the period, their crude bases and capitals curiously cut in one piece with the shafts. This opening intrudes into the head of the arch underneath it and belongs to the ninth-century tower. The tower room behind it served perhaps for a sacristan who could keep watch from there over the altar and its treasures, perhaps for a priest who could thus say the night offices without descending into the nave, or was perhaps a chapel.

9 St Mary, Stow, Lincolnshire: interior, looking east
The vast early eleventh-century arches before us, some thirty feet high, surpass those of any other surviving Saxon church in scale. They form part of a true crossing, where nave, transepts and choir are all of equal height – a feature found in only one other Saxon church. They must have supported a crossing tower, perhaps of wood; when a new tower was built in the fourteenth century they were strengthened by extra pointed arches, of which one is visible. From their plain impost blocks, which seem to rest on powerful attached shafts, spring broad roll-mouldings (like

those at St Bene't's, Cambridge, pl. 18) and on the outermost order, a band of palmette.

Ruinous after the Conquest, the great church was given a Norman nave and chancel, the latter restored by Pearson in 1853–64. The font in the foreground, harmonizing with the early work in its bold geometric shapes, dates from the thirteenth century.

10 St Mary, Breamore, Hampshire: south chapel arch
11 St Nicholas, Worth, Sussex: north chapel arch seen from the chancel
Both Breamore and Worth, late Saxon churches dating from the beginning of the eleventh century, assume the cruciform plan, but their low side chapels cannot be described as true transepts. The simple shape of the narrow opening into the surviving chapel at Breamore (now the vestry) concentrates the eye on the oddly placed caterpillar-like ornament on the right-hand impost and on the inscription incised on the arch, which proclaims in Old English, 'Here the covenant is manifested to you.' The form of the letters relates them to the reign of Ethelred II, 979–1016. The bellropes reveal the presence of the central tower.

At Worth the cruciform plan does not include a central tower. The photograph conveys the exceptionally beautiful chiaroscuro of this interior and the great monumentality of the chancel arch with its unusual semicircular piers and cushion capitals. It also concentrates the atmosphere of the church by focussing on a wall where every architectural detail is Saxon.

12 All Saints, Earls Barton,
Northamptonshire: west tower
13 St Peter, Barton on Humber, Lincolnshire: central tower
Both towers are late Saxon, and both belong to a plan in which the ground floor of the tower served as the nave. That at Barton on Humber is the centre of a three-celled design, the western unit of which can also be seen in the photograph. The 'long-and-short' work of the quoins at Earls Barton contributes to the dazzling display of ornament with its emphatic alternation of upright stones with flat slabs projecting

beyond the angles to clutch the walls. The arcade motif on this tower shoots inconsequentially above the string-courses, and the match-stick triangular heads of the upper row, divorced from their pilaster strips and exuberantly repeated, turn into diamond patterns. At Barton on Humber the thin pilasters of the upper arcading rest in a highly unorthodox fashion upon the arch tops of the lower arcade.

Beside the twin windows at Earls Barton with their curiously ringed, ornamental balusters and on the arches of the openings encircled consecration crosses can be seen. The procedure for consecrating churches had been decided by Theodore of Canterbury in the seventh century: there were to be twelve consecration crosses on the inside walls of the building and twelve on the outside, the latter being peculiar to English ritual.

14 St Mary, Sompting, Sussex
The variety of late Saxon architecture is well illustrated by a comparison of this elegant and sparsely adorned early eleventh-century structure, crowned by its unique gabled spire of Rhenish inspiration, with the ornate towers at which we have just been looking. Sompting's long central pilaster strip, rounded rather than flat above the string-course, and the low placing of that single string-course, idiosyncratically carved with a miniature arcade motif, enhance the vertical emphasis, as does the cutting back of the horizontal stones of the quoins to the width of the upright stones – true long-and-short work. The local flint of which the tower is built was once entirely hidden by the now patchy plaster. But the locality of the structure is also proclaimed by the shingles (thin oblong pieces of oak split, not cut, from the wood) covering the spire.

15 St John the Baptist, Inglesham,
Wiltshire: Virgin and Child
16 St John, Barnack, Northamptonshire:
seated Christ
17 St Mary, Sompting, Sussex: an abbot or bishop blessing
18 St Bene't, Cambridge: detail of the tower arch
The Inglesham and Barnack pieces, one

rustic, the other carved with sophisticated mastery, one sweetly unaffected, the other majestic, are both distinguished by a humane and gentle naturalism. The image of the Inglesham Virgin and Child over-shadowed by the large hand of God the Father is surprisingly fresh: the Child sits deep in his mother's lap, one little hand resting on her sleeve.

The rhythmically linear relief at Sompt-ing has an utterly different, expressionist allure. The exaggerated hands, the great eye, the extraordinary distortion of the arms, the arresting design of the capitals from which the leaf-sprouting arch curves like a strong tendril, and the magically unsupported stance of the crozier all suggest that the sculptor was copying an illustration in a manuscript.

Different again in its rude, outlandish strength, the detail from the arch of St Bene't's exhibits the same mixture of fierce energy and fantasy as the text of the contemporary *Anglo-Saxon Chronicle*, the oldest manuscript of which is close at hand in the library of Corpus Christi College. The immense weight of the bizarre capital is vigorously and ingeniously counteracted by the tensed beast springing up from the entablature instead of resting on it. The cat-like creature is surely intended as a lion, emblem of St Mark and appropriate guardian of openings, as it was thought to sleep with its eyes open.

2 St Peter with St Cuthbert, Monkwearmouth, Co. Durham

3 *St Lawrence, Bradford on Avon, Wiltshire: view across the nave from the north porticus*

4 *St Wystan, Repton, Derbyshire: crypt*

5 St Lawrence, Bradford on Avon, Wiltshire: chancel

6 *All Saints, Wing, Buckinghamshire: apse*

7 St Mary, Deerhurst, Gloucestershire: *window in the west wall of the nave*

8 All Saints, Brixworth, Northamptonshire: *west wall of the nave*

9 (opposite) St Mary, Stow, Lincolnshire, *looking east*

10 St Mary, Breamore, Hampshire: south chapel arch

11 (opposite) St Nicholas, Worth, Sussex: north chapel arch seen from the chancel

12 *All Saints, Earls Barton, Northamptonshire*

13 St Peter, Barton on Humber, Lincolnshire

15 *St John the Baptist, Inglesham, Wiltshire*

16 *St John, Barnack, Northamptonshire*

14, 17 (opposite and below) St Mary,
Sompting, Sussex

18 *St Bene't, Cambridge*

CHAPTER TWO

The Norman and Transitional era

THE NORTHMEN FROM WHOSE FURY the Litany prayed for deliverance in the ninth and tenth centuries had become French-speaking Christian traders, operating from their base in Normandy, by the millennial year when Christendom expected the end of the world. As traders and expeditionary forces they extended their sway as far as Sicily, the Holy Land, Constantinople, Russia and Central Asia; and from all these places strange motifs were brought back to north-western Europe by artists and craftsmen.

The term 'Norman architecture' suggests that the Normans created a new type of architecture in England. But both the Anglo-Saxon and Norman styles were variants of Continental Romanesque architecture. In Anglo-Saxon buildings the Romanesque elements were interpretations of echoes of the Roman tradition rather than of the tradition itself; but the form of Romanesque which the Normans had already adopted for their churches, monasteries and castles in France sprang more directly from Roman sources. The Normans' forceful translation of the Roman manner eventually led, towards the end of the twelfth century, to the tentative use of a revolutionary constructional system based on equilibrium, on the balanced thrust of masses, thus entirely departing from the Roman method which depended on the principle of inert stability.

Norman Romanesque is conspicuous by its mass and solidity. Norman towers – often enriched by arcading as at Castor, Northamptonshire, and sometimes marked by a small staircase turret, as at New Romsey, Hampshire – are impressively broad and heavy. A Norman interior is unmistakable with its round-headed, moulded arches and window-openings and its huge cylindrical pillars or piers with moulded, cushion or volute capitals. Such features distinguish the vast new cathedrals and abbeys and are grandly displayed in many a parish church. *19*

26–29

The most imposing Norman parish churches are aisled, cruciform buildings. Their builders favoured a central tower and built it not upon walls pierced by openings in the Saxon manner, but upon piers and arches. They reintroduced the apse of the basilican plan (though they also built many square-ended chancels) and they developed a tripartite plan consisting of nave, central choir and eastern sanctuary; Kilpeck, Herefordshire, is an unaltered example of this plan. *36* Occasionally in this type of church the tower was raised over the choir, as at Iffley and Stewkley. But this plan did not persist any more than the circular plan, of which five examples remain: St Sepulchre at Cambridge, St Sepulchre at Northampton, the Temple Church in London, Little Maplestead in Essex, and the chapel of Ludlow Castle. They were modelled on the Church of the Holy Sepulchre at Jerusalem and were chiefly associated with the Knights Templar.

37

19 St Kyneburga, Castor, Northamptonshire

Compared with Anglo-Saxon work Norman Romanesque has a 'grand manner': meant to impose on the conquered Anglo-Saxons and on the peripheral Welsh and Scots; conceived and boldly executed by men of furious energy and animal drive; as deliberately and monumentally, almost menacingly, massive in ecclesiastical as in military structures. The first two Williams' Tower of London and St Alban's Abbey epitomize the double drive of the Normans in Church and State in the land now added to their Continental realm. The Conquest was as much one of ideas of State-craft (centralized administration and law, the Continental feudal system of land tenure and military obligations) as of Church-craft (more centralized administration through a hierarchy on the Roman model); and new men were everywhere put over the native Anglo-Saxons, in the Church in England as in the shires and counties and smaller estates down to the new fiefs of knights and esquires. By 1080 Wulfstan of Worcester was the only remaining Anglo-Saxon bishop, for although eight out of fifteen pre-Conquest bishops and many abbots were left in possession after 1066, it was only for the duration of their lives, and William appointed no Englishman to an English see. New itinerant justices went to new assizes to administer both the old common law of the Anglo-Saxons and the new Norman feudal and kingly laws. New traders and merchants settled in English ports and towns. Nor were these 'new men' all Normans: Italians, Bretons, true Frenchmen, Flemings, even Spaniards came into England with Norman overlords.

Though by the date of Domesday Book, 1086–87, not more than 25,000 'foreigners' could have settled in England – about one in fifty of the population – and though a big Anglo-Saxon village consisted of no more than a hundred souls, this light leavening of the English lump achieved within two generations an unprecedented rate of progress in almost all walks of life: agriculture, trade, building, law, fiscal and financial management, and civil administration. The costs were a sharp reduction for the first two generations in the Anglo-Saxons' standard of living, as the Norman upper crust of some 1,500 of the larger new landlords took their rents and dues in kind from their newly organized manorial village lands; the burden of the new civil and military services; a fall in the general status of women; a manifest tightening of military rule, evident in the hundreds of new castles hastily erected; and a vast extension on all sides of the feudal *corvée* or forced-labour system, not merely on the land (where the Anglo-Saxon lords had exacted their obligations of labour and produce) but wherever workmen and craftsmen could be marshalled for the huge, ubiquitous, civil, military and ecclesiastical building programmes which were going on simultaneously. 'We labour to heap up stones' bitterly complained Bishop Wulfstan of Worcester.

The vast number of parish churches built or enlarged by the Normans were designed not only for the accommodation of a growing population, but to accord with changes in ritual. The new Continental, more Roman clerics brought in more ritual, better Latin, more colour, better chanting and singing, to appreciate all of which clearer vision and hearing were necessary from the people's nave into the new or enlarged choirs and sanctuaries. The main entrance to the church was 25   now almost always by a doorway on the south side of the nave at the west (see above, p. 17). There was often a less elaborate portal on the north side as well, especially if the manor house or the greater part of the village lay to the north of the church, as at Witney, Oxfordshire. This north door was popularly known as the Devil's door and was left open at baptismal services, so that evil spirits which might be in a child could pass out. Where a western door was retained from an older church, as at Worth, Sussex, or was included in a new plan, as at Castle Hedingham, Essex, it was reserved for processional purposes. It was for this purpose, too, that the spacious Norman aisles were planned. A few Saxon churches, as we have seen, were aisled, but the magnificent arcades of such churches as St Peter's at Northampton and Melbourne, Derbyshire, gave an 42, 29 altogether new dimension to the visual poetry of the parish church. The aisles provided a processional path and a means by which worshippers could reach any part of the church without disturbing those already in their places. Another advantage of aisles was that altars dedicated to tutelary saints could be placed against their eastern walls.

In spite of the shock of the Conquest and William I's intention of reforming the English Church, the organization of the parish church and the life of the village priest were not drastically changed. Owing to his low social position, the priest was not disturbed by an influx of foreign clerks. The priests who appear in the earliest assize rolls, those of Northamptonshire and Lincolnshire, are actively engaged in cultivating their glebes. Among them are Robert of Blyborough, who in 1202 was convicted of digging a ditch which impaired the working of the mill of one of his parishioners, and an anonymous parson of Stainby in Lincolnshire, who was so old that neither he nor anyone else could remember who had presented him.

As a rule the parish priest remained married, though some bishops tried to enforce the rule of clerical celibacy introduced by Lanfranc, the Norman archbishop of Canterbury. Hugh of Lincoln required Alan, vicar of Ashwell in Hertfordshire, to execute a bond undertaking to pay 30 marks if he again cohabited with his mistress, Annora. But the married state of the village priest – of whom so much is heard in the twelfth-century Life of Wulfric of Haselbury, written by John, Abbot of Forde – is never questioned. The spoken language of the foreign settlers remained French, while written Anglo-Saxon gave way to Latin. Of John's many anecdotes which give us a vivid portrait of Britric the priest, one must suffice to conjure up the atmosphere of the period. Wulfric had cured a dumb man. The saint was surprised that Britric seemed annoyed rather than awed by the miracle. 'Lo,' said Britric, 'I have served you so many years, but today I have proved that it is vain, for to a stranger, for whom it would have been quite sufficient for you to have loosened his tongue, you have given the use of two languages, while to me, who when I come before the bishop and archdeacon am compelled to be silent like a dumb man, you have not given the use of French.'

Among the innovations which did affect the parish priest was the granting of churches to monasteries. This resulted in the practice called the impropriation of a church, whereby the monastery kept the greater part of the church's endowment for itself (including the tithe of crops and stock) and left the priest with the offerings to the altar and the lesser tithe. It was a custom which made monasteries rich and kept parish priests poor until after the Lateran Council of 1215, when the Pope decreed that the parish priest must be given a decent living through the institution of vicarages, which should be the freehold of the priest who served the church. The ubiquity of vicarages today shows how widespread impropria-tion became after the Conquest.

The Normans admired (or at least employed) Anglo-Saxon craftsmanship; for in many of their rebuilt parish churches we can see traces of the best Anglo-Saxon work – the smaller, narrower windows; the long-and-short quoins visible at crossings and ends; sculpture and carvings. In Gloucestershire there is a remarkable concentration of parish churches embodying Saxon and Norman work – Daglingworth, Elkstone (with a remarkable chancel with single east window and roof boss), Bibury, Stratton, the two Duntisbournes, the Cerneys, Ampney St Peter, Bagendon and Quenington, all near to each other. By the first quarter of the twelfth century, two generations since 1066, new parish churches of great scope *32* and variety were being built. Tickencote, Rutland, is one example, with two eastern bays made into one by sexpartite stone vaulting, and a vast chancel arch, magnificently if simply axe-carved in five orders of beakheads (virtually unknown outside England), cables, billets, and rough geometrical zigzag designs, typical of *23* Norman work. St Mary at Patrixbourne in Kent has a massive tower with a south portal set in a slightly built-out gable with a niche and carving of the Lamb of God, and three round-headed east windows with a round window over. Nearby *20* Barfreston is on a simple two-cell plan, but with magnificently carved south portal and tympanum, blind arcading at the east end with a splendid wheel-window above, no tower, but one of the finest corbel-tables round any early church left in *29* England. Melbourne in Derbyshire is a French rather than an English example of Norman work, with a western narthex and two towers and a three-light Norman rood-screen. One must emphasize the elaboration and diversity of treatment of the semicircular tympana above portals of Norman parish churches. The sinuous Tree *33* of Life at Kilpeck, Herefordshire, and the wildly imagined beasts and birds with tails turning into interlacings surrounding it, the vigorously linear St Michael and Dragon at Moreton Valence, Gloucestershire, and the extraordinary beasts battening on the Tree of Life at Dinton, Buckinghamshire, are among a body of early twelfth-century work which seems to have been inspired by old Norse carvings and recalls the wiry fantasies of some Scandinavian jewellery. The more sophisticated tympana of the second half of the century, like those at Elkstone, Gloucestershire (Christ in Majesty) and Barfreston, Kent (Christ in the act of blessing) recall the richly decorated churches in France south of Poitiers.

36, Fonts exhibit the same variety, whence we can again deduce that the *38–41* craftsmanship of Anglo-Saxons was put at the service of their new masters; witness those at Avebury, Wiltshire, and at Stewkley and Stone, both in Buckingham-shire. One group of fonts, however, is definitely associated with the Continent – those made of lead. That at Wareham, Dorset (with a hexagonal bowl) shows figures in bold relief in its arcading and recalls fonts in the Dordogne region; some authorities indeed think it may have been imported from France. Black marble carved in Belgium was used for fonts finely worked in low relief, seven of which survive: that at East Meon, Hampshire, with its reliefs of Creation and Fall, is typical in the firm, harsh style of its figurework. These lead and Tournai marble fonts, like building-stone from Caen, testify to the greater cross-Channel trade and traffic in Norman times. Of all Norman church furniture and fittings the fonts show the widest variation of motifs and styles: round and tub-shaped, on square bases or pedestals, supported or not by pillars at the corners. A remarkable group of Norman stone fonts is in Herefordshire and neighbouring counties, at Eardisley, *39, 40* Rowlstone, Chaddesley Corbett and Castle Frome – the last carved with the Baptism of Christ and signs of the Evangelists, and resting on prostrate figures. The work is characterized by interlacing patterns of great boldness which (like the Kilpeck carvings) suggest Norse prototypes. *34*

As we see them today, Norman church interiors give a poor impression of their original appearance, for the polychromatic paintings with which they were covered are virtually lost. Some idea of the way in which these murals transformed an austere nave and chancel is given by the restored decoration at Copford, Essex, which spreads over the whole of the original building. The spirited painting of the Judgment on the west wall of the nave at Chaldon, Surrey, is another survival.

Throughout the twelfth century society in England was fast changing. After the chaotic times of the first Norman kings ending with Stephen, the Angevin dual kingdom of England and Normandy-Aquitaine was comparatively stable and well administered, particularly under Henry II, despite the murder of Becket. Between, say, 1150 and the downfall of John after Magna Carta in 1215, new secular ideas of royal government and administration were accompanied by equally new Cluniac, Cistercian and other ecclesiastical innovations and reforms. The estates of monasteries, collegiate churches, priories, cathedrals and other foundations not only became enlarged by legacies and donations: the ecclesiastical landlords themselves became leading improvers of agricultural methods. Trade and towns grew, thus expanding markets for the villages' surplus produce; the old Anglo-Saxon self-sufficiency of the village and its lord or lords gave way to the first production for other markets than the insulated manorial area; and the monks, especially Cistercians, took the lead in pushing back the primeval forest and woodland that still covered much of England and held villages apart. Former waste was turned into arable land and, above all, into sheep-runs.

By 1150 there were already between 450 and 500 monasteries in England. Small wonder that kings began to look askance at the extension of ecclesiastical power and properties, especially in a feudal system where almost all wealth and military strength came from the village and its fields. Yet prosperity was growing with more population and trade. The wool trade enlarged ports in eastern and south-east England; communications by land and sea improved; there was much more coming and going, not only by merchants and traders but also by an increasing class of clerics and ecclesiastical authorities, and by civil servants and judges (whose staffs still consisted mainly of clerks in holy orders) and the feudal forces of the king and his nearest baronial vassals. It would have been remarkable if such change had not brought an equally striking change in architecture and its attendant arts and crafts. It did indeed.

The great change can best be traced from the Norman style proper to the Transitional, and thence to the true Gothic of the first Early English style, by following the transition from round-headed arches or windows to those which rise to a point. Sir Christopher Wren gave the name 'Gothic' to this 'barbarian' style of architecture because it so blatantly departed from the classical tradition. The term 'Transitional' applied to the period between about 1170 and 1220 is somewhat misleading, for it gives the impression of steady progress into full Gothic. The first, true, full Gothic in England's churches, the Early English style, was in use in new building, and spreading rapidly, by 1180. But both long before and long after, certain elements of French Gothic – pointed arch and rib vault – were used in what remain basically *Romanesque* structures. For this reason 'Transitional' is employed for such building in the few decades preceding and succeeding 1180.

The pointed arch (supporting thrusts from above and sideways better than rounded arches) and the rib vault (permitting vaults of stone over wider spaces than the old narrow groin vaults and barrel vaults) are found very early in Norman architecture. As early as 1104 they were used (in a vault no longer there) at Durham Cathedral, and its famous stone-vaulted nave was completed by 1133. Yet it took another two generations for the implications of these structural innovations to be realized. By pointing *all* the arches of any space to be vaulted, pointing them a bit higher or lower as needed, the vault could be of uniform height throughout; whereas with round arches the diagonal arches across any bay must either rise higher than the arches at the sides, or else start to spring from lower down the sides. This realization, coupled with one other – that the weight of any vault is concentrated at the points from which the arches or ribs spring – led to full Gothic. That style could be epitomized as holding up higher walls, and vaulting over wider spaces, by means of counter-thrusting members; these members rise to points, countering each other's thrusts, the thrusts being carried in turn to foundations spread out widely enough to dissipate them. Hence of course the use of buttresses, which in Norman churches appear as fairly thin pilasters running down walls to the foundations, but in Gothic buildings project far with many offsets, sometimes even 'flying', to make of some Gothic cathedrals a network of muscles *outside* the body.

24
91

This excursus into church architecture is necessary because the Transitional style clearly displays the revolution in architecture and its attendant arts and crafts caused by the slow realization of what vast edifices pointed arches made possible. It was not until French Gothic entered England with William of Sens' rebuilding of Canterbury choir between 1174 and 1184 that this realization suddenly burst on architects, master-builders and masons in England, and spread to the small churches. The striking contrast between Norman and Gothic can often still be seen in one and the same church in all parts of the country: for example at Anstey, Hertfordshire, an older rounded chancel arch is juxtaposed to pointed arches in nave and clerestory, and at Faringdon, Berkshire, the nave arcade is Norman and Transitional but crossing, transepts and chancel are Early English.

Often one finds the Transitional pointed arches reposing on Saxon or Norman columns or piers; often as heads to windows, though it is yet too early for stone tracery. It is always rewarding to look up and all round to follow, by the arches, this great transition to Gothic. It is worth comparing Melbourne, Derbyshire, or *29* Adel, near Leeds in Yorkshire – both pure Norman work – with say, the choir at New Shoreham, Sussex, or the nave arcades at Avebury or Faringdon. There are *47* only fifty to sixty years between the two kinds of work; yet they are worlds apart in appearance, in the feelings they evoke, in the imaginative spirit inspiring their creators, and in the outlooks on life of those who conceived and executed them.

At Shoreham, Sussex, we have two Norman churches – St Nicholas at Old Shoreham, St Mary de Haura (from *havre*, harbour) at New – which admirably *46, 47* show the development from Saxon through Norman and Transitional to full Gothic work. Old Shoreham is on a simple aisleless cruciform plan with central tower and (originally) apsidal ends to both transepts and chancel, the typical Norman central tower being squat and now shingle-covered. The western walls are part Saxon; the Norman structure is early, about 1100; it has a rare Norman tie-beam (possibly the old rood-beam) with carved billet decoration over the west arch of the crossing; and its builders used the base of the ninth- or tenth-century Saxon tower in the new nave, beyond which opens the Early English to Decorated chancel. New Shoreham, built later of Caen stone and finished in the Transitional style, is vast but – unlike some of the greater Norman churches – was always a parish church, in this case for an already thriving seaport. The original nave has disappeared, leaving only the tower and transepts and the unusually large choir, rebuilt in the last quarter of the twelfth century, which is one of the grandest in any parish church. Its south arcade has Norman compound piers; but the north arcade has alternately round and polygonal columns and their capitals show the transition from Romanesque pseudo-Corinthian to Early English leaf carving. Above both arcades rise pointed arches, and between them and the (by now much higher) clerestory the extra stage of a triforium is introduced, normally seen only in major churches or cathedrals. Foreshadowing the full Gothic style, wall-shafts now run up the piers to support the new stone rib vaults, probably dating from the early thirteenth century, which are braced outside by flying buttresses.

Another set of contrasts can be seen in the central tower of the cruciform Norman church at Castor, Northamptonshire: a typical piece of Continental Romanesque work, massive, with elaborately carved and coursed stone panels and lights, continuous round-arched arcading and heads to the lights, rich groundwork of chevron-like panelling above the lower arcade, and fish-scale ornament above. This is capped with an abnormally stocky Early English octagonal spire rising from a fretted stone parapet of later date; but if you look closely at the stone-coursing of walls and tower you see old Saxon work in the former, and fine late Norman jointing (with thin lines of mortar) in the latter. Nor are Castor and New Shoreham singular in portraying so clearly this great transition and transformation of the English people and their churches between the tenth and thirteenth centuries. The story of the great change – as great as that from ancient rural England to modern industrial urban England – is writ large in parish churches.

Notes on the plates

19 St Kyneburga, Castor, Northamptonshire: central tower
This thrusting image embodies in the weather-resisting Barnack limestone of the district many characteristics of Norman church-building. The tower is the central feature of a true cruciform design (consecrated, an inscription records, in 1124) and combines mass with rich ornament. The whole surface of the structure above the roof-line corbel-table is covered with scale patterns and varieties of rhythmic arcading. It is typical that the central three-light window of the lower stage should be more deeply recessed and more elaborately moulded than the blind flanking arches (though with the same billet motif), and that the three bell-openings should be flanked by blank arches.

The openwork parapet and short broach spire were added in the fourteenth century.

20 St Nicholas, Barfreston, Kent: detail of the south door
Norman ornament is so profuse and so striking that it dominates our image of the style even though it was a comparatively late development. The decoration was often concentrated on the south door of a church, but seldom more sumptuously than at Barfreston. Artists of the late twelfth century in the south-eastern district of Kent were in touch with Continental developments, and the work at Barfreston recalls the richly ornamented churches of the Charente in western France. But the French model has here been translated into a purely English idiom. The linear, nervous quality of the very low relief which gives a marvellous unity to the teeming detail is as original as the spirited inventions which fill the medallions.

21 St Mary, Haddiscoe, Norfolk: view from the south

22 St Andrew, Bishopstone, Sussex: view from the south-west
23 St Mary, Patrixbourne, Kent: view from the south-west
All three churches are memorably sited and are wonderfully expressive of the chalk and flint of the South Downs and of East Anglia. Patrixbourne and Bishopstone are built of flint with Caen stone for quoins; the designer of the picturesque Norfolk pebble tower dispensed with quoins, for which no local stone was available, by making the structure circular. The Haddiscoe tower combines Saxon and Norman details and like Bishopstone represents the earliest phase of Norman influence in England. While the twin triangular-headed bell-openings at Haddiscoe proclaim its Saxon origin, the billet ornament around them is a Norman embellishment. The decorative battlements and checkerwork are fifteenth-century additions.

The beautiful tall unbuttressed tower of Bishopstone was not built until the twelfth century, so its date makes it Norman, but apart from the bell-openings the tower is wholly Saxon in conception. Its proportions are quite different from those of the short, squat tower of Patrixbourne (to which the shingle spire was added later). The severely plain walls of this structure accentuate the richness of the south door, decorated with five orders of plant-entwined inventions in shallow relief like those at Barfreston. A relief of the Lamb appears in the niche above the door and the whole is enclosed by a steep gable of such slight projection that it is more like a pediment. The same feature occurs at St Margaret at Cliffe, not far away.

24 St Andrew, South Lopham, Norfolk: view from the north
The cow-parsley foams at the foot of a tower which for size and design is an

astounding object in a gentle uneventful landscape. It is unusually lofty, even without the fifteenth-century flushwork parapet, and unites dignity with caprice in the variations and irregularities in the grouping of the plain arcading and in the treatment of the piers. The wide, shallow angle buttresses are typical Norman versions of this feature. The tower was added to a Saxon church early in the twelfth century.

25 St Mary Magdalen, Tixover, Rutland: west tower and south porch

The photograph shows the dramatic siting of this pale limestone church in the midst of cornfields away from the road. The tower has all the mass, the fortress air and the static character associated with Norman architecture. And unlike that of South Lopham it is remarkable for the precision and control of its austere and noble design. The calculated contrast between the three plain arches and square piers of the bell-openings and the continuous arch below, enclosing a shafted arch with another continuous arch of zigzags within it, is extraordinarily satisfying. The circular clerestory windows were a happy Victorian addition to a totally dark early twelfth-century nave.

26 St Mary the Virgin, Lindsell, Essex: interior, looking towards the chancel
27 St Michael, Onibury, Shropshire: interior, looking west
28 St Peter, Little Barrington, Gloucestershire: north aisle

Whereas the sparsity of ornament at South Lopham and Tixover is an indication of date, the touching simplicity of Lindsell and Onibury is wholly rustic. St Mary the Virgin stands among farm buildings and it is its atmosphere rather than its architecture which enchants. The small interior, strikingly pale because largely built of clunch, a soft, easily worked chalk stone, is almost square and seems to be filled with arches. The one in the foreground of the photograph springs from a quatrefoil pier of Early English character and we look across the south aisle towards the plain Norman chancel arch. The huge squint beside it was cut in the fifteenth century to allow the congregation in the aisle to view the elevation of the Host. The shuttered

opening in the north wall of the chancel enabled a twelfth-century anchorite who, like many another at that time, lived in a rough cell attached to the outside wall, to receive the Sacrament. The priest at the time of Domesday is described as a poor villein. The first priest whose name is known, 'a certain clerk named Henry, skilled in medicines', was presented at about the time the chancel arch was built, in 1154.

Yet more remote and diminutive, the Onibury interior with its bare arch, relieved only by insignificant zigzag and pellet decoration, and its homely tie-beam roof, is surprisingly impressive and solemn. The little west gallery and the lamps were added by Detmar Blow in 1902.

At Little Barrington differences of style are resolved into an almost classical harmony by the crisp, clear detail of the beautiful Cotswold stone and by the commanding curves of the two late twelfth-century arcade arches sweeping up from short cylindrical, scallop-capitalled piers.

29 St Michael and St Mary, Melbourne, Derbyshire: interior, looking east

The aisled nave of Melbourne is part of the most ambitious parish church example of the Norman cruciform plan, with a central and two western towers, an apsidal chancel and apsidal chapels. The small market town owes this superb building to the fact that the manor and rectory were granted to Aethelwold, Bishop of Carlisle, at the time of his appointment in 1134. The surge of the mighty arches is accentuated by the application of a single motif, the chevron, and it is made to move to a slower, more majestic measure by the wall-shafts rising from the pier capitals.

30 St Mary, Iffley, Oxfordshire: west front

As eloquent a vindication as Melbourne of the vital role of ornament in architecture, this integrated composition depends on the consistent use of the beakhead and chevron motifs on mouldings which are continuous, without columns and capitals – a not uncommon device in the late twelfth century. Surprisingly, the rose window and the blind window in the gable which provide such effective accents were Victorian insertions, though Buckler, who installed the rose in 1856–57, had found the outline of a blocked circular window. The side windows in the gable, cut into when the roof was lowered in pitch in the seventeenth century, were restored in 1823.

31 St Mary, Iffley, Oxfordshire: detail of the west door
The detail brings out the contrast in treatment between the bold beakheads and chevrons and the shallow, linked medallions (compare Kilpeck, pl. 34), that show the symbols of the Evangelists and signs of the Zodiac. The ferocious beakhead motif, Scandinavian in origin like the Normans themselves, is more widely diffused in England than anywhere else.

32 St Peter, Tickencote, Rutland: chancel arch
The experience of stepping for the first time into the constricted interior of Tickencote is sensational. The bizarre and bedizened chancel arch, strangely distorted by its own weight, seems to fill the entire church. Created about 1160–70, it displays as many as six orders, adorned with billets, chevrons, crenellations and imaginative versions of the ubiquitous beakhead, varying from stylized leaves to the amazingly diverse inventions based on plants, animals and human forms on the third order.

33, 34 St Mary and St David, Kilpeck, Herefordshire: details of the south door
There is a certain resemblance, already remarked, between the outer ornament of the Kilpeck arch and that at Iffley (pl. 31), but here it looks like a translation into stone of some opulent necklace of gold, jewels and enamels. The schematic, inverted heads serving as links are especially remarkable; they look Celtic, and the distinctive regional style of the work has been ascribed to Celtic as well as Viking and West French influences.

The writhing sculpture on the jamb shaft again invites comparison with metalwork, in particular the great bronze Gloucester Candlestick of similar date in the Victoria and Albert Museum, and Viking metalwork and wood carving. The symbolism of the two puppet-like knights entangled in snaky coils is unclear, but the salamander on the capital represents the power of passing

unscathed through temptation, while the dragon in the form of a fat serpent swallowing a small snake typifies Christ's descent into Hell.

35 St Mary and St David, Kilpeck, Herefordshire: sheila-na-gig and cat from the corbel-table
The man who carved the corbel-table running all round the exterior of the church was not the sophisticated artist of the south door, but his naive fantasy and humour and the bold simplicity of his forms are among the chief delights of Kilpeck. The sheila-na-gig, an ancient fertility figure, surprisingly appears on churches scattered across the country, always outside.

36 St Mary and St David, Kilpeck, Herefordshire: interior, looking east
Despite the extravagant decoration of the arches and ribs of the sanctuary apse it is the chancel arch in the foreground of the photograph which determines the exotic character of this small three-celled church, probably begun shortly after 1134. A remarkably concentrated vitality radiates from the figures of the apostles growing one above the other out of the shafts. Their position has parallels on the Continent, but in style the figures are closer to English ivories of the period. At the left side of the arch is a curious Norman holy-water stoup, its bowl like a fat belly clasped by two arms.

37 All Saints, Staplehurst, Kent: south door
The construction and ornament of medieval church doors are invariably interesting, but this prodigious and curious display of twelfth-century hammered ironwork is uniquely evocative of an ancient craft and its associations. The conspicuous C-shapes in the design recall crescent symbols which, like the smith's art, are rooted in magic rites older than Christianity: like iron itself, they had the power of averting evil. At the same time they refer to St Clement, the patron of smiths. His emblem is an anchor, and this appears on the door in natural conjunction with a rudimentary boat and sea creatures.

38 Holy Trinity, Lenton, Nottingham: font
39 St Mary Magdalene, Eardisley, Herefordshire: font

40 St Michael, Castle Frome, Herefordshire: font
41 St Andrew, Foxton, Leicestershire: font
The font, less subject to change and restoration than the main fabric and less frequently replaced than other furnishings, is often the most ancient and most interesting object in a church. The earliest of the four shown here is the great square font at Lenton, astonishingly encountered in an undistinguished Victorian interior. Its size, like that of the three other huge bowls, reminds us that immersion was the rule. It is probably of the same date, about 1110, as the rich Cluniac priory on the site, of which it is the sole survival. Perhaps the Cluniac connection accounts for the intriguing character of the reliefs: on the right in the photograph is the Crucifixion; on the left (clockwise from the top right) the Resurrection, the three Maries at the Tomb and the Ascension.

The two Herefordshire fonts belong to the same local school of sculpture as the work at Kilpeck (pls. 33, 35), though later in date, and are masterpieces of that style characterized by strange rope-like folds. The carved drama of the bowl is in each case framed above by a bold plait decoration, traditionally believed to be a charm against evil, and below by a taut knot design at Eardisley and at Castle Frome by a loose, snaky briar-like interlacing which climbs up the bowl to take part in the action. At Eardisley long coiling tendrils impart an air of nightmare to the struggle between two knights, resembling those at Kilpeck (pl. 35), and separate them from the figure of a saint clasping a book. The Castle Frome font, carved about 1170, is a more mysterious work. The subject on the side seen here is the Baptism, with God's hand above the head of Christ, while to the left the angel of St Matthew holds out his gospel in a great rush of wings. The water is seen as a circle of ripples, in which fish symbolize the souls of Christians. But what above all distinguishes this marvellous object are the dark beings lying crushed beneath its weight, demons subdued by the power of the Church, a motif found in Italy.

The Foxton font, ornamented with one of the most appealing of Norman motifs, the interlaced arcade, immediately attracts attention on account of the splendid idiosyncrasy of the artist's method of adapting the square bowl to an octagonal base: the corner shafts suddenly curve inwards as though cut loose from their feet.

42 St Mary, Sutterton, Lincolnshire: capital
43 St Peter, Northampton: capital
44 All Saints, Faringdon, Berkshire: capitals
The quatrefoil design of the pier at St Peter's is one indication of the break from old traditions during the second half of the twelfth century. The admirably controlled, wiry design of the coiled tendrils and the treatment of the mythical beasts and palmette leaves are even closer to metalwork than the south door ornament at Kilpeck (pl. 33), and suggest goldsmith's work.

The imposing capital at Sutterton, its square abacus indented at the corners, ornamented with interlaced arcading and nailhead and supported by a crude form of the foliage which was to distinguish early Gothic architecture, is typical of the mingling of Norman and new forms seen in late twelfth-century churches. A more elegant display of this tendency is seen in the range of capitals on the crossing arch shafts at Faringdon, which date from about 1200. Here big, stiff-stalked foliage of the Early English variety is most interestingly juxtaposed to the palmettes and trumpet scallops which preceded it, while one curious, leaf-sprouting form of the scallop shows a stage in the metamorphosis of the Norman into the Early English capital.

45 St Peter, Little Barrington, Gloucestershire: detail of the south porch arch
The innermost moulding of this arch is adorned with the gentle, pyramidal four-pointed star ornament known as the dogtooth, the most characteristic Early English motif, but it is aggressively overlaid by the boldest Norman chevrons, exaggerated into jagged beakheads, all the more alarming because severely abstract. It is an almost hysterical assertion of the Norman style just as it was about to yield to a new mode, at the end of the twelfth century.

46, 47 St Mary de Haura (of the Port), New Shoreham, Sussex: view from the south-west, and interior, looking east
Blanched by salt winds, this soaring

composition has a silvery pallor which relieves the concentration of its powerful forms. It is only a fragment of the original vast church built about 1130, the nave of which was ruined in the Civil War. The truncated west end, towards which we are looking, was rebuilt in the early eighteenth century, so it is uncertain whether the reset doorway arch was always pointed, as are the enclosing arches of the tall belfry windows and the arcade arches of the interior.

The congregation is now confined to what was originally the choir, rebuilt about 1170 in an ornate Transitional style. The alternately round and octagonal columns of the north arcade, seen here through the earlier tower arch of proud and contrasting simplicity, are already carved with Gothic stiff-leaved foliage, while the arches are pointed. And of the openings in the gallery above three are pointed and two are trefoil-headed, while the east end combines Norman with Gothic openings. The quadripartite vault (rare in a parish church), built of clunch, the chalky local stone, is altogether Early English in feeling.

20 St Nicholas, Barfreston, Kent: detail of the south door

21 St Mary, Haddiscoe, Norfolk

23 (opposite) St Mary, Patrixbourne, Kent

22 St Andrew, Bishopstone, Sussex

24 (opposite) St Andrew, South Lopham, Norfolk   25 (above) St Mary Magdalen, Tixover, Rutland

26 *St Mary the Virgin, Lindsell, Essex*   27 *St Michael, Onibury, Shropshire*

29 *(opposite) St Michael and St Mary, Melbourne, Derbyshire, looking east*

28 *St Peter, Little Barrington, Gloucestershire: north aisle*

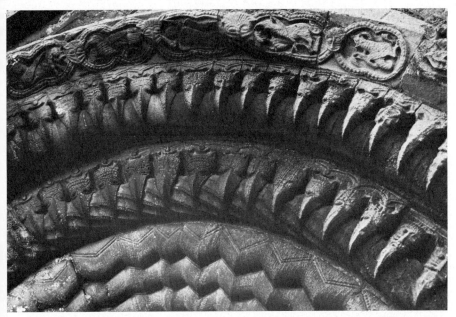

30, 31 (opposite and above) St Mary, Iffley, Oxfordshire: west front and detail of the west door

32 St Peter, Tickencote, Rutland: chancel arch

33–36 *St Mary and St David, Kilpeck, Herefordshire: details of the south door (left and below) and corbel-table, and view of the chancel (opposite)*

37 (opposite) All Saints, Staplehurst, Kent: south door

38–41 (above and below, left to right) Fonts at Holy Trinity, Lenton, Nottingham; St Mary Magdalene, Eardisley, Herefordshire; St Michael, Castle Frome, Herefordshire; and St Andrew, Foxton, Leicestershire

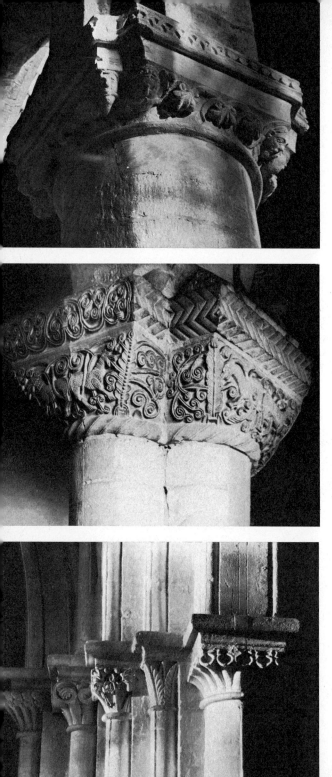

42 St Mary, Sutterton, Lincolnshire

43 St Peter, Northampton

44 All Saints, Faringdon, Berkshire

45 (opposite) St Peter, Little
Barrington, Gloucestershire: detail of
the south porch arch

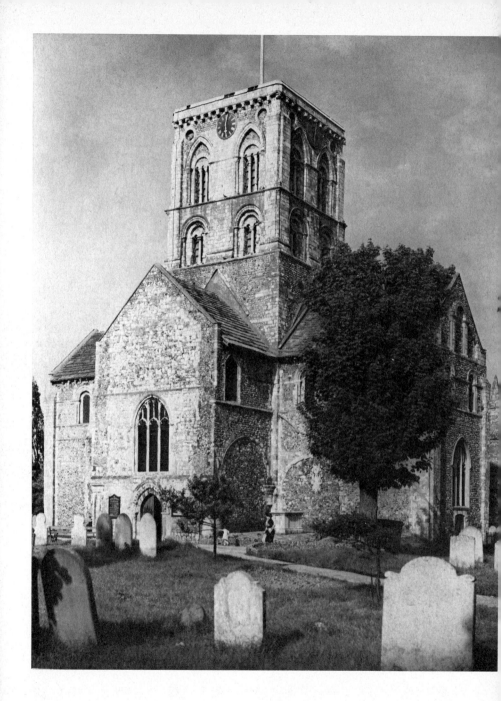

46, 47 St Mary de Haura, New Shoreham, Sussex: view from the south-west and interior, looking east

CHAPTER THREE

From 1200 to the Black Death:
Early English and Decorated Gothic

AT THIS POINT WE MUST PAUSE to take stock of the everyday life of the English people in their villages and small towns. The barely 1½ million souls in England at the time of Domesday Book became, through the Norman-Angevin-Plantagenet reorganizations, reforms and innovations, more than double that number in the 282 years between the Conquest and the Black Death. In those ten generations the villages remained much the same in number, but they grew both in population and in extent by 'assarting' new land from the vast forests, led by the example of the big ecclesiastical foundations. Whereas at Domesday Book London had only about 10,000 inhabitants, York and Norwich 6,000 each, and Oxford and Ipswich only 5,000 each, these biggest English towns had nearly doubled in size, and London more than tripled, in the interval. On the bigger estates of the Church, and to some extent on the smaller but still extensive estates of the lords and barons and knights, huge flocks of sheep were now grazing. Early thirteenth-century charters speak of pastures for 300 sheep at Barnetby and Norton in Lincolnshire, and for 500 sheep 'by the long hundred at Swinethorpe'. English wool was at a premium; the first English cloths were beginning to find markets at Continental fairs (hitherto only the wool had been exported); and with this growth of internal and external trade went merchants, financiers, shipowners, navigators, as well as clerics and potentates.

England had been covered with new churches, big and small, mainly between 1150 and 1250, after which it was largely a matter of pulling down and rebuilding them. As W. G. Hoskins points out, in *The Making of the English Landscape*, it was during these hundred years that 'the division of England into ecclesiastical parishes was completed (at least until the rapid expansion of the northern and Midland towns during the Industrial Revolution) and the parish church arose as a visible symbol and centre of a new community'.

'A new community' is an exact description of what the great transition had accomplished before the Black Death struck in 1348: not only the entire English community, which had already absorbed its French-speaking kings and courtiers, but even more so its various component little communities in their villages and embryonic towns. Villages grew into small towns, and small villages into larger communities, all with new churches, sometimes with more than one parish and church in each. East Anglia, the Fenlands, and the Lincolnshire-Cambridgeshire-Huntingdonshire-Rutland area started the large-scale sheep and wool trade

67

48 St Lawrence, Didmarton, Gloucestershire: north transept, now a vestry

through east coast ports; Kent, Sussex and Hampshire dealt with the nearby
Continent; the good stone belt reaching from Northamptonshire through
Oxfordshire and the Cotswolds to Wiltshire, Dorset and Somerset turned to
98, 103 sheep-raising and produced the magnificent 'wool churches' somewhat later. In
stoneless Essex, Middlesex, Buckinghamshire, Surrey, in the bare and under-
settled far north, the Welsh marches, and remote Devon and Cornwall the
building of new parish churches lagged.

Along that belt of stone just mentioned church spires began to lift their heads
above the less-forested landscape during the second half of this great church-
building epoch – that is, in the Gothic period proper. Villagers and burgesses vied
with each other in raising and embellishing parish churches which now seem far
too big for the population of that epoch, and far too big for the church-going
population of today. The magnitude of both the Church's and its parishioners'
offerings, converted into stone and furniture and fittings of all kinds, including
church plate, was colossal. Parish churches shot up almost cheek-by-jowl in
town and city parishes – over 100 in London with barely 40,000 inhabitants before
1348, over 25 in big towns like Norwich or York with only 8,000 to 10,000 people.
As better trade, communications and agriculture brought villages nearer to each
other, churches grew bigger and more imposing. Hoskins has calculated that in
tiny Rutland alone, on that belt of stone, there were over 50 medieval churches,
one to every 250 souls, though each capable of holding many more. Such emula-
tion in building, out of a low standard of life, cannot have been solely due to pride,
even pride in local achievement. The desire to glorify God in an age of deep belief,
and in an era of short and uncertain human lives, is apparent on all sides in these
new and imposing parish churches; for their naves were the people's first and only
communal buildings. Beside the hovels and mean manorial halls the churches, in
their stone and coloured finery, seemed Heaven on earth, eternal. Moreover (we
forget) there was only one belief, and virtually no expressed disbelief.

As the parishioners were responsible for building, maintaining or enlarging
their nave, it (and its aisles, porches, chapels and other portions) continued to serve
secular as well as religious purposes (see above, p. 16). This dual character is
reflected in the duties of the churchwardens, whose office had been instituted by
the Council of London in 1129. In addition to raising and administering the funds
necessary for the upkeep of the fabric and services and to prosecuting offenders
against ecclesiastical law – the few recalcitrants who would not go to church, or
blasphemed, or scolded, or otherwise scandalized the neighbours – the churchwardens collected the rents of lands left to the Church, farmed the Church
stock of sheep and cattle, and sold wool and cheese and other gifts in kind. They
also organized the Church Ales (see above, p. 16), when ale was brewed in the nave
in the parish utensils and consumed there by the jovial and contributory
parishioners.

There was no heating in churches till modern times. The floor was strewn with
rushes or dried bracken to keep feet warm and to dry off the ubiquitous mud, at a
time when there were no drains (except round the church gutters, and not always
then) and when every thatched hovel had its roof-drainage pool before its door,

into which all human and animal slops were thrown. There were no seats in churches: all stood, trying to glimpse the mysteries and to comprehend the (ill-spoken and ill-understood) Latin beyond the rood-screen in the chancel or sanctuary. But along the nave or aisle walls there usually ran a ledge to which the weak might retire to rest upright, still technically on their feet: this is the origin of the phrase 'to go to the wall'. Nave columns and piers sometimes also afforded such ledges. There was always much coming and going in naves and aisles, much noise, much smell, as – whether a service was going on or not – men and women on their way to or from the large open fields where they laboured for their manorial lord, or for themselves on their own plots, went in and out to pray, or be shriven, or hear the Mass.

Masses continued to be said by the priest every day throughout the day, from early each morning, and in winter in the dark when the labourers would be on their way to the fields, and townsfolk already about their business or crafts. There were independent craftsmen in every village, too: carpenters, wheelwrights, millers, smiths, whose skills are still attested in many an old church. It was the customary, unwritten, sometimes even written, law that every adult parishioner should attend Mass daily, and High Mass on Sundays and the many other 'holy-days', which numbered some forty in a year. Traders, merchants, clerics, judges and other travellers would commend themselves to St Christopher before setting forth, which is why his image, generally big, usually appears inside churches on the north wall facing the south porch, so that he and the Child could be seen from the door – as he can still be seen at Pickering in Yorkshire, Baunton in Gloucestershire, Abbess Roding and Lambourne in Essex, and Bartlow in Cambridgeshire.

It was, as mentioned above, an age of belief; religion dominated everyday thinking and behaviour. Yet ordinary village folk did not take communion more than three times a year, if as much. A 'state of Grace' was not frequent. Faith was a matter of ritual, cult, practices, superstition; conformity to all of these was general; no one dared to be 'out-standing', unless it were a case of (rare) witchcraft or (even rarer, until after the Black Death) heresy.

The parish priest was one of the people, perhaps a bright boy from some village whose priest had selected and furthered him through the nearest monastic, cathedral, or other major church's school. He had a wife and family up to the thirteenth, even into the fourteenth, century, after which the rule of celibacy in Roman priesthood became both general and obeyed. Even then he might still keep a mistress by whom he had children, illegitimate, many of them handing down to posterity the surname 'Parsons' or 'Maudling'. Priest and parishioners were allotted and cultivated in common, with the village ox-teams and workers, their particular plots, 'furlongs', long thin rectangular strips of land, by which the whole community throve or – rarely – went hungry. Through the long winters, when work was lighter, all lived on the precious salted-down beef or other meat, which needed the rare salt and even rarer spices to make it palatable; and, above all, on bread and milk, cheese, and animal fat. Fresh-water fish was a staple item of diet. Honey provided sweetening; for although we read of Henry III buying 34 pounds of sugar for his own use at the rate of 9d. a pound, sugar only became accessible with the increase in trade and remained out of reach for most people till the seventeenth century

The parish priest embodied the Church and in time became known as the parson, the chief 'person' of the parish. He had double the ordinary villager's strips of land, and often a little holding near his dwelling: it was church land, the glebe (from the Latin *gleba*, soil) referred to in the preceding chapter. Impropriation, already described (p. 39), often meant that most of the yield of the village's or manor's lands would go to the governing body of the possessing foundation, who in turn would select and nominate the parish priest (who thus fared poorly). This was the origin of a number of the splendidly constructed tithe-barns which have survived from the period. The same system gave rise to 'rectors' – ecclesiastical and lay – and the vicars or curates appointed by them to 'care' for the villagers' souls: a complex organization persisting to this day in the appointment to 'livings' in the Church of England.

Parishes were small and compact in towns, becoming more compact as the towns' populations grew. They were naturally wider for villages, becoming widest in the extreme north, which William I had laid waste and which never recovered until the Industrial Revolution in the eighteenth century. From 1066 until that century England was a rural land in which very few village communities exceeded 250 to 300 souls, however wide the parish and however numerous the agricultural manors in it. One can reckon the average village at fewer than fifty households, bound together by everyday work and life, shared risks and natural hazards, early deaths in each household, lack of sanitation and medical aid, and by the shared belief which alone could provide any succour or comfort. Whether at work or on holy-days the sound of church bells recalled these folk to worship and alarms, to work or play, to wake or sleep, or to dowse their fires in their thatched hovels at curfew (*couvre-feu*, 'cover the fire') at each day's end. The little Sanctus bell, often in its special bell-cote, was always rung at the saying of the Sanctus at the beginning of the Mass, and again at the consecration and elevation of the Host. During the period covered by this chapter ringers began to experiment with new ways of hanging the church bell so that its sound could be controlled. Before the fourteenth century church bells were normally hung on a simple spindle – as they mostly still are on the Continent. The first improvement was made about 1300 by mounting the bell on a wooden quarter-wheel, the spindle serving as the axle with the rope attached to the rim of the wheel. Even more control was gained when the bell was mounted on a half wheel. Most parish churches by this time had two or three bells, and more came later.

As churches were enlarged, by longer chancels or the addition of aisles, it became harder for parishioners to see and hear the officiating priest; so one often finds in churches which have been enlarged (especially those later given transepts 26 and a central tower or big crossing) 'squints' cut obliquely through piers, pillars or walls to allow sight of the altar in the chancel. Another, still unexplained, characteristic of this growth stage of parish churches is what is called the 'low side window', often wrongly termed 'leper's window', generally low down in the outer wall of the choir or chancel and generally on the south side. As it often had a

hinged opening below, it may have been for the ringing of a Sanctus bell by hand
to alert people outside (by no means lepers, as there could never have been so many
in England) when there was no Sanctus bell-cote and no other way of announcing
the Sanctus.

We followed in the last chapter the transition from Norman to Gothic. Early
English is the first pure Gothic style. It achieves its lightness in contrast to earlier
styles mainly by fine lines, a linear pattern of ribs and wall-shafts to support the
new stone vaulting in the greater churches, windows with many mouldings, many
columns and shafts often clustered together, and crisp, deeply undercut foliated
capitals. Most obvious naturally are all the new tall and narrow pointed arches. The
carved mouldings favoured by the Normans have given way to a series of thin rolls   *29, 55*
and hollows etched with sharp lines of shadow and adorned at most with the
dogtooth ornament, a hollowed-out pyramid pattern. An air of delicate restraint
strikes one in any church exemplifying the Early English style. Its charm and
refinement are partly due to the use of new tools, to the substitution of chisel
and gouge for the axe, the results of which are already apparent in late Norman
and Transitional carving, and partly to the perfect union between architecture and
decoration. Though its forms are conventionalized, the ornament seems to grow
vigorously and naturally out of the surrounding structure. The monk Gervase,
writing of the differences between the Norman choir of Canterbury and its Gothic
replacement begun in 1174 by the Frenchman William of Sens, points out with
pride: 'In the old capitals the work was plain, in the new ones exquisite in sculpture. . . . There the arches and everything else was plain, or sculptured with an axe
and not with a chisel. But here almost throughout is appropriate sculpture.'

Eaton Bray, Bedfordshire, is a delight because behind its Perpendicular exterior   *50, 52*
it contains fine unrestored Early English elements. The arcades spring from
remarkable corbels (especially on the south, of about 1220), and have luxuriant
foliage capitals and beautiful mouldings (especially on the north, built some fifteen
years later). There is a typically chaste font, very different from the fantastically
sculpted fonts of Norman churches, supported by pillars at the corners and with
foliage carving; and on the south door the necessary wrought-iron reinforcements
take the form of gracefully scrolling tendrils.

One of the finest examples of the new Gothic style of parish church building is at
West Walton, Norfolk, begun in 1225. Externally both the body and porch and   *55, 65*
the unusual massive detached tower-gateway to the churchyard appear more like
northern French work than like Salisbury Cathedral, the masterwork of Early
English, with which they are nearly contemporary. The blind arcading outside,
though linear in a vertical way, seems a little heavy, conveying something still of
the more massive Transitional work. But once inside, one is struck by the width,
lightness, length and delicacy of the nave and its arcades, with their slender four-
shafted piers and foliage capitals, the latter the only sculptural ornaments. The
shafts stand free of the central column, a peculiarity of the Early English style, but
are tied to it by the moulded bands half-way up. They were originally of Purbeck
marble, the dark fossil-filled limestone popular throughout the thirteenth century

(see, for instance, the play of dark against light at Salisbury and Lincoln Cathedrals), but some have been replaced by wood, and most have been whitewashed.

56, 57   Almost as impressive an example of Early English is Uffington, Berkshire. Built on a cruciform plan that is relatively rare for a parish church, it was finished in the middle of the thirteenth century, with a central tower on a square base. The Early English device of triple lancet windows shows to perfection in the transept ends, as it does in the east window of Stanton Harcourt, Oxfordshire, and in the multiple pattern in the famous Mitton Chapel at Bredon church, Worcestershire.

The light, delicate, restrained Early English style gradually evolved into the more ornate, more naturalistic Decorated style which, from around 1290 to the Black Death in 1348, spread through half a century of Plantagenet rule. Here again one must warn against assuming a discontinuity between styles. Just as Norman and Transitional elements persisted into the Early English style, so the Decorated retains earlier elements and very occasionally foreshadows the later Perpendicular forms. Another factor also now appears, stemming from the greater prosperity, more intense trade and town life, firmer administration at home and warlike successes abroad under the gifted Plantagenet monarchs. It is a factor reinforced from the Continent, where Englishmen's (and women's) skills in civil and military arts and crafts were forging that high renown they later attained – a process brought to a climax with the victory at Crécy on the eve of that Black Death which caused such a setback throughout Europe.

From the Continent came ever more colourful, elaborate and imposing ritual and ceremony in churches. As towns grew in prosperity, and agricultural improvements pushed up yields for lay landlords and ecclesiastical foundations, more display and grandeur (and higher standards of consumption in the villages) were accompanied, it seems, by a greater fear of death and the after-world. Perhaps this intensifying fear lies behind the greater elaboration of the Decorated style of church building and furnishing. The sharp eye can detect it at once, in contrast to the simpler linear motifs of the Early English mode, in many innovations and

72–74   embellishments: the appearance of more elaborate window tracery in stone; the
58,   uprush of richly crocketed stone spires (often over older towers) that made
60–61   English churches famous and infused the English landscape (and later the English landscape school of painting) with a special charm; and the fast-multiplying oratories, chantries, chapels and altars inside churches, imparting yet another impulse to enlarge the buildings, and foreshadowing the almost rectangular, even-

p. 243   sided church which was the ultimate achievement of the peculiarly English Perpendicular style.

Window tracery came into English architecture about 1240 and, though its development can be more completely followed in cathedrals and greater churches, parish churches can show superb examples. Plate tracery, evolved by piercing the solid masonry between a pair of lancets, occurs for instance in the tower of Clipsham, Rutland, at Kilworth, Leicestershire, St Giles's at Oxford, and in the aisles at Stone, Kent; though it is comparatively rare. Bar tracery, in which the tracery is composed of a framework of stone mullions rather than cut out of the solid, was at first a simple matter: cusped circles were inserted in the heads of lancet-shaped windows. But it swiftly grew more elaborate, especially with the Decorated introduction of odd numbers of lights – three or five instead of two or four – which tended to prevent the simple multiplication of circles, and to create complex intersecting patterns in the window-head. By about 1290 the S-curve had appeared, a result of the same impulse which gave rise to the cult of the ogee arch, and opened the way for those writhing, flame-like forms that characterize Decorated tracery in its Curvilinear or Flamboyant phase. (The earlier, simpler form of bar tracery is often, equally logically, called Geometrical.) 72, 73

Didmarton, Gloucestershire, displays a modest three-light window with a quatrefoil placed between two pointed trefoils. Splendidly ornate late Geometrical–early Decorated windows adorn the south aisle at Leominster, Herefordshire. Their complex tracery includes triangle shapes with straight edges forming a circle at the top, as well as cusped five-pointed stars, and it is further enriched by an incrustation of ballflowers, larger or smaller according to their position on the enclosing arch or on the most delicate mullions. What happened when the flowing element superseded the Geometrical can be seen at its simplest in reticulated tracery, such as that in the east window at Ludham, Norfolk, where a net of flickering shapes half-fills the opening. At Witney, Oxfordshire, the Curvilinear tracery of a window-head is echoed below the window in two tomb-recesses of unusually spiky pattern, which, like the windows at Leominster, are trimmed with ballflower. The tracery of the Decorated style takes forms of almost infinite variety and complexity; and such was the fascination of these forms for artists of the time that we even find them carved in wood, on choir stalls, and in stone, as on the font at North Hinksey, Berkshire. 48
74

72

80

86

Such complexity would seem improbable in three dimensions; yet it was achieved at least once in a parish church: at St Mary Redcliffe, Bristol, which flowered at the outset of the fourteenth century into 'one of the most famous, absolute and goodliest parish churches in England' – in the words of Queen Elizabeth I. The unique north porch is in plan a hexagon, vaulted with a six-pointed star, and has a strange, angular doorway with heavy foliage carved about it in contortions suggestive of seaweed. 76

p. 74
66, 67

This porch was built with an upper room, a feature which became common during the fourteenth century. The room was put to various uses: parochial registers and documents were kept in it, it might be used as a chapel or as a library, saintly relics might be preserved there, as at Grantham, Lincolnshire, sometimes the sexton slept there and occasionally it was used as a schoolroom, as at Shifnal, Shropshire. The upper room at St Mary Redcliffe is elaborately decorated and is famous through its association with the poet Thomas Chatterton: here he spent days brooding over old manuscripts, becoming so strongly moved by his medieval surroundings that he felt compelled to write medieval poetry which he then presented as the rediscovered work of a fifteenth-century Bristol poet, Thomas Rowley. Only one of the 'Rowley Poems' had been published when Chatterton committed suicide, in 1770, at the age of seventeen.

Nowhere are the salient features of the Decorated style more nobly preserved

The north porch of St Mary Redcliffe, Bristol (see p. 73), built c. 1320–25. It consists of a normal square chamber next to the church (top), preceded by a unique hexagonal room with a complex star vault. From the hexagon large buttresses project, ending in three points, each of which itself terminates in three shafts (see pl. 66).

than at Patrington, Yorkshire, which was built out of the profits of the Humber *64, 68*
export trade in wool and cloth. It is distinguished by the unity of its design
throughout and by the grandeur of its cruciform plan that incorporates aisled
transepts. The impressive columns, no longer composed of individual shafts
grouped about a central core, but presenting a multi-shafted, complex image,
diamond-shaped on plan, carry arches of greater span than those of Early English
naves. The windows – that include a rare, small rose window in the south transept
gable – display the flowing, leaping patterns of the period in delightful variety.

The close-clustered foliage and flowers wreathed about the Patrington capitals
are typical of the luxuriant forms which have taken the place of the stylized and
clearly articulated Early English ornament. Realistic rendering of oak, vine,
sycamore, briony and eglantine is accentuated by the extraordinary inclusion of
torn, tousled and blistered leaves – seen also at St Mary Redcliffe. The finials *66, 67*
adorning the exterior of Patrington are conspicuous for the serrated outline
formed by a repeated, sprouting ornament like budding foliage, known as a
crocket. This is a favourite device of the Decorated style, which is as instantly
proclaimed by the ballflower motif, a globular form enclosed by three petals,
which superseded the Early English dogtooth ornament for filling the mouldings
of arches and windows, as at Ledbury and Leominster in Herefordshire.   *74*

Patrington is the most harmonious parish church composition in the Decorated
style, but many other remarkable churches exhibit its distinguishing features,
including Higham Ferrers and Finedon in Northamptonshire, Heckington and St   *60*
Botolph's at Boston, both in Lincolnshire, and Yaxley in Huntingdonshire. The   *95*
church of Ottery St Mary, Devon – a curious sprawling design with a long chancel
and towered transepts – is one of the most unforgettable expressions of the style. It
was rebuilt from about 1337 by Bishop Grandison of Exeter, who had purchased it
from Rouen Cathedral. Apart from its unusual shape it is remarkable for the
variety of its vaults. The chancel shows a boldly curving pattern of transverse   *82*
arches and liernes and big rosettes in a rib system which is, however, purely
decorative. In the Lady Chapel, by contrast, the ribs form a fine trellis punctuated
by splendid bosses with carved figures, among them St Anne and the Virgin, the
Assumption of the Virgin, St John the Baptist, the Last Judgment and Bishop
Grandison himself. The carvers almost certainly came from Exeter, where similar
fine work appears in the nave vault of the cathedral.

Furniture and fittings in parish churches of this period have survived only
patchily. However, two survivors among the paintings of the Early English and
Decorated periods are outstanding: the wall-painting of the Virgin and Child at
Great Canfield, Essex, and the retable at Thornham Parva, Suffolk, showing the   *78*
Crucifixion flanked by saints. The Great Canfield Virgin and Child is drawn in red
and yellow ochre with fine flowing lines and tender expressiveness, and the
enclosing painted arch is ornamented with stiff-leaf forms. The Thornham Parva
retable is a highly sophisticated composition of subtle rhythms and swaying figures
set against a background of patterned gold, which has evoked comparison with
work of about 1300 in Westminster Abbey. Another retable, comprising seven
panels depicting the Annunciation, the Passion and various saints, is in St Michael-

at-Plea, Norwich; and a series of fourteenth-century murals, including a Doom over the chancel arch and the Ascension on the north clerestory wall, were uncovered earlier in the present century at Pickworth, Lincolnshire.

Among surviving wooden screens of the period, those of Patrington, Yorkshire, and Castle Hedingham, Essex, are little altered. More novel and much more
79   arresting screens of stone fill the chancel arches of Stebbing and Great Bardfield in Essex, unexpected images in a stoneless district. These stone screens date from the time of the Black Death, and a comparison of their voluptuous, rhythmic design with that of the timber screens of earlier date to survive, such as the Early English structures at Kirkstead in Lincolnshire and Stanton Harcourt in Oxfordshire, with their simply cusped arches and attenuated shafts, shows clearly the development which had taken place between about 1200 and 1350.

Sedilia – two- or three-stepped seats occupied by the celebrant, the deacon and the subdeacon during the singing of certain parts of the Mass – became permanent features of the south wall of the chancel from the twelfth century onwards. The ogee-shaped canopies of the sedilia at Patrington in Yorkshire, Hawton in
81   Nottinghamshire, Nantwich in Cheshire, Heckington in Lincolnshire, and Cliffe in Kent, encrusted with ornament, are among the showpieces of the fourteenth-century masons. Hawton and Patrington also each boast an Easter Sepulchre, used in Holy Week ceremonies to re-enact the Burial and Resurrection of Christ. The Sepulchre at Hawton is carved with reliefs of the Resurrection and sleeping Roman soldiers in ogee-arched niches.

75   At Ottery St Mary one of the oldest eagle lecterns in the British Isles stands with outstretched wings on a globe bearing the arms of the donor, Bishop Grandison. It is of gilded wood. Another oaken eagle of about the same date is preserved at
191   Astbury, Cheshire, but most lecterns are of later date and are of brass.

Many typical fonts of the thirteenth and fourteenth centuries remain. The circular or polygonal bowl on pillars, as at Stow, Lincolnshire, is especially characteristic of the Early English style, and is found also at Leighton Buzzard, Bedfordshire, and at St Mary's at Cricklade, Wiltshire. But octagonal bowls became increasingly common, usually raised on a stepped platform, as at Patrington, Harpenden in Hertfordshire, and Wantage in Berkshire. Fonts of the Decorated period are more lavishly ornamented than the earlier bowls, very often showing ogee-shaped and crocketed arcading, as at Wendover, Buckinghamshire, and Market Bosworth and Ratby, Leicestershire; or adorned with Decorated
86   tracery as at Weobley, Herefordshire, and North Hinksey, Berkshire.

We know from cathedrals and greater churches that many fine memorial sculptures were executed during the thirteenth and fourteenth centuries; some sepulchral effigies exist in parish churches which reveal the same high quality. The popularity of commemorative sculpture was growing apace. During the thirteenth century figures of knights and churchmen were for the first time separately carved and laid on a tomb chest. Thirteenth-century cross-legged knights lie at Walkern, Hertfordshire, and at Stowe-Nine-Churches, North-amptonshire, in a lively posture peculiar to England. More dramatic than either is the knight of about 1320 at Aldworth, Berkshire, who leans on one arm

with updrawn legs as if about to rise, while Sir Oliver de Ingham at Ingham,   *89*
Norfolk, lying on a bed of stones with a formidable lion at his feet, turns as if in
sleep, with an uncanny effect of realism. Knights with their ladies at
Threckingham, Lincolnshire, and Fountains, Yorkshire, rest more calmly, flat on
their backs, exhibiting early fourteenth-century fashions in gowns and armour.
Guilds of marblers, masons and alabasterers had sprung up to meet the demand for
effigies, which were rarely portraits, and generally no more than a stereotyped
figure made personal by the use of heraldry and inscriptions. If a stone monument
proved too costly, the memorial took the form of an engraved brass. The earliest
examples of monumental brasses date from the thirteenth and fourteenth centuries, are life-size, and represent nobles and priests. Such are Sir John Dabernon
at Stoke d'Abernon, Surrey (1277), Robert de Bures at Acton, Suffolk (1302), and
the famous Sir Robert de Septvans at Chartham, Kent (1306). Of the fourteenth   *88*
century also are the finely incised figures of Sir John de la Pole and his wife under
an ornate buttressed arch at Chrishall, Essex, and the intricate engravings of Sir
John and Lady Creke (dated 1325) at Westley Waterless, Cambridgeshire, as
slender and elongated as the saints of the Thornham Parva retable.   *78*
    Externally the most striking innovations of the thirteenth and fourteenth
centuries in parish churches were in tower design. There is a good list of famous
English towers and spires, by counties, in Tyrrell-Green's *Parish Church
Architecture*, the best naturally occurring in the belt of good stone-quarries running
diagonally across England from the south-west. Some Early English towers
resemble those of the Norman period in outline, but the surface arcading has
pointed rather than rounded arches. A group of fen-country churches shows this
feature, with fine examples at Leverington, Tilney All Saints, Long Sutton and
West Walton. But the most important development of the aspiring, essentially
vertical Early English style is the setting of a spire of octagonal shape upon a square
tower. At its simplest, the awkward join between an octagonal tapering spire and
the square top of the tower is made by means of smooth half-pyramids of masonry
– broaches, hence the term broach spire – at the four corners. A noble example is
the spire of Raunds, Northamptonshire. Ketton, Rutland, near the famous   *59*
quarries, boasts a spectacular fourteenth-century broach spire with tracery in its
lucarnes and sculpture at the tips of the four broaches and round the base of the
spire. Sometimes the broach is used in conjunction with angle pinnacles, as at
Grantham in Lincolnshire and Newark in Nottinghamshire, where pinnacles   *61, 58*
appear on the tips of the broaches. At Higham Ferrers, Northamptonshire, there   *60*
are no broaches: from the corner pinnacles openwork flying buttresses spring up to
the richly crocketed spire. Finally at Patrington, Yorkshire, the junction of tower   *64*
and (Perpendicular) spire is masked by an octagonal corona in the form of tall
arcading.
    There is a rare example of a free-standing belfry at Pembridge, Herefordshire,   *63*
which has an octagonal base of rubble and ashlar and a shingled roof rising through
two square timber stages (also shingled) to a pyramidal peak, and a wonderful
interior of open beams, trusses and struts. This church, like that of Blackmore,
Essex, with its timber tower rising in diminishing stages, shows the influence that

local materials exerted on construction and style. Many villages boast
extraordinary spires on towers of all kinds, tall and thin, short and squat – as in the
Home Counties, especially Buckinghamshire, Middlesex and Hertfordshire,
where a distinctive small and very narrow spire, the 'Hertfordshire spike', evolved;
farther afield, especially in the north and the West Country, towers become
70 majestic, massive, and often (as along the border with Scotland, or near sea-coasts
in Devon, Somerset and Cornwall, where piracy flourished) defensive.

The Decorated period was more or less punctuated by the disastrous plague known
as the Black Death, which struck in 1348 and returned twice before 1370. It made a
great hiatus in English life (as it did to life on the Continent), in towns and, far
worse, in villages, of which many disappeared. There was a sudden surplus of
cultivable land and lack of hands to work it. Serfdom received its death-blow.
After the plague's worst course had been run inside a few years, wages soared;
landlords, lay and ecclesiastical, tried to exact the old obligations in kind (free
labour on their land, free produce) and failed, but only after great violence and
outright rebellions – of which Wat Tyler's, only a generation after the plague, was
the biggest. In the towns the priests who remained at their posts, trying to help
their parishioners, died in droves; in Norwich, two-thirds of the parish priests
succumbed. Scratched on a wall inside the west tower at Ashwell, Hertfordshire, is
a Latin verse, roughly translatable:

> 1350 – Miserable, savage, crazed,
> Only the worst of people remain as witnesses,
> And to cap all came a tempest
> With St Maur thundering over the earth.

(Another of the graffiti at Ashwell comments, 'The quoins are not jointed aright –
I spit at them.' A third is a drawing of Old St Paul's in London.)

When church-building, trade and agriculture revived, a new, still more
elaborately ambitious mode, which had been slowly evolving in details during the
Decorated period, burst forth in full splendour: the Perpendicular style, a uniquely
English invention.

Notes on the plates

48 St Lawrence, Didmarton, Gloucestershire: north transept
Some of the churches shown in this book are monuments of awe-inspiring grandeur: here we encounter, not for the first time, but in a more domestic guise, the vein of homely rural poetry which so often transfigures a village church with no great architectural pretensions. Now used as a vestry, this interior, with its wooden staircase going up to a bell turret, its irregularly paved floor and a bunch of wild flowers on the ledge of the simply traceried window, partakes of the character of a modest early manor house.

49 St Andrew, Weston, Staffordshire
The elegance of the finely pointed lancets is accentuated by their background of large sandstone blocks and by the massive bulk of the tower with its broad buttress. The single lancet of the lower stage, with its hood-mould above the arch, shows the simplest form of the window which is the distinctive feature of the Early English style. A more complex arrangement appears in the bell stage, where the actual openings are enclosed by the central arch of a shafted triplet of lancets. The heads of the arches take the form of open circles, and show the emergence of the trefoil-headed shape seen also in the delightful early thirteenth-century door.

50, 52 St Mary, Eaton Bray, Bedfordshire: south door and south aisle, and north arcade
The atmosphere of thirteenth-century architecture can be savoured at its purest and most intense in the interior of Eaton Bray. The south arcade, with its polygonal piers, tightly curled stiff-leaf capitals and ornate corbel supporting simply chamfered arches, dates from about 1220. Some fifteen or twenty years later the north arcade was built (pl. 52), and its looser foliage is echoed in the tousled leaves of the font, seen beyond the door.

The exquisite scrolled ironwork completely covering the face of the door is typical of the mid thirteenth century. It may be the work of a great medieval smith, Thomas de Leighton, who made the grille

for Queen Eleanor's tomb in Westminster Abbey and the doors of the churches at Leighton Buzzard and Turvey in Bedfordshire.

The north arcade piers, rising from characteristically low, ringed bases, consist of eight shafts about a central core, some of them, as can be seen in the photograph, slightly detached and imparting greater momentum to the surge of forms up to the stalks of the foliage, tightly pressed against the capitals before breaking into large, curling leaf clusters. Then the same upward movement, reinforced by multiple roll-mouldings, begins again. The truncated mouldings springing at right angles to the arcade formed part of arches across the aisles, a highly unusual arrangement.

The big fire-hook which can be seen through the pillars of the north arcade is one of many specimens still stored in parish churches. With it fires were extinguished by the summary process of pulling down the burning house, which in the Middle Ages was usually built of timber and thatch or mud and thatch, unless it was an important structure.

51 All Saints, Icklingham, Suffolk: chests and hassocks
The reed hassocks are of the same material as the thatch of the church's nave roof. The scrolly ironwork of the chest in the foreground exhibits the same Early English character as that of the Eaton Bray door (pl. 50). Every parish church once had its great chest for the preservation of its churchwardens' accounts, parishioners' wills and, after the Reformation, of the parish registers. Plain, unornamented chests like the one on which the hassocks are placed were common in all periods.

52 St Mary, Eaton Bray, Bedfordshire: north arcade. See pl. 50

53 St Leonard, Kirkstead, Lincolnshire
This church adjoins the remains of Kirkstead Abbey and was once the abbey's chapel *ante portas* (outside the gates), which partly accounts for its aesthetic perfection. It

dates from about 1230 and, tiny though it is, it is nobly and most memorably expressive of the Early English style in its every detail. Even the screen with its trefoiled arches, a rare survival, sustains the theme. The colour of the interior is as unforgettable as the simply arched forms of the sexpartite vault, the shafted, deeply splayed lancets and the contrasting luxuriance of the bursting foliage of the capitals: the arches and vaulting ribs are of an ochre yellow stone, emphasizing their pure shapes against the whitewashed walls.

54 St Candida, Whitechurch Canonicorum, Dorset: shrine of St Wite

The photograph affords a glimpse of the variation of the Early English theme which makes St Candida remarkable: the clusters of enchantingly light, ringed and detached shafts, unusually high-based and with capitals diversely carved with forms like unfolding fern fronds rather than leaves. The most conspicuous object in the picture, however, is the shrine of St Wite. It is the only medieval shrine in England, apart from that of Edward the Confessor in Westminster Abbey, which still contains the bones of a saint. St Wite's remains attracted flocks of pilgrims in the Middle Ages and the shrine was famous also as a place of healing. Afflicted arms and legs or some article belonging to the sick person would be thrust into one of the oval openings in the lower part of the tomb.

The shrine probably dates from the thirteenth century, but St Wite herself, whose identity is obscure, is thought to have lived in the sixth century and to have come from Brittany to marry the Prince of Cornwall. Legend confused the Saxon name of Wite with the Old English word *hwite*, 'white' (whence Whitechurch), which was later translated into Latin as Candida.

55 St Mary, West Walton, Norfolk: interior, looking west

This view of the nave from the chancel takes in the whole superbly poised and graceful structure: the unifying elements are at once apparent. The chancel arch and the arcade arches are enlivened by the same multiple mouldings and the aspiring rhythm of the arcade is encouraged by the imaginative

addition of another arcade above it for the clerestory, where each alternate arch frames a window. Here, as elsewhere in the church, the shafts stand delicately detached; originally of dark Purbeck marble from Dorset (as they are in Salisbury Cathedral), some of the West Walton shafts have been replaced with wood, and most are unfortunately whitewashed. The capitals are richer, more undercut versions of those seen at Eaton Bray (pl. 52). The west window is a Perpendicular replacement of an Early English lancet composition.

56, 57 St Mary, Uffington, Berkshire: exterior from the south-east, and north transept chapel

The church gives an unusually consistent impression of the grave simplicity and serenity of the style which reaches its great climax at Salisbury and Lincoln. The chaste lancets with their plain hoodmoulds, single, paired or in triplets, the buttresses with their thin string-courses and knife-like gablets, the elegant shafted piers with their rounded, unadorned capitals and the sharply pointed arches all announce their thirteenth-century origin so harmoniously that the divergent note struck by the reticulated window at the west end of the chancel is hardly noticed. Nonetheless this cruciform church is highly individual. The octagon surmounting the square central tower is wholly unexpected. Its top storey turns out to be an eighteenth-century addition. Perhaps the mid thirteenth-century builders planned a spire.

The transept chapels, with their eccentric angular gables and windows, may possibly reflect seventeenth-century alterations to the Early English chapels, of which we see an interior (pl. 57). Such chapels built to house altars previously set against the walls were once common: these are among the few survivals. Every altar in a medieval church had its piscina or drain nearby, into which the rinsings of the ceremonial ablutions were poured, to sink away into consecrated earth. Here the piscinas are small but surrounded by a striking deeply cut double moulding, which catches the light. Sometimes they are combined in a single design with seating for the clergy (pl. 81).

The door beside the south-east chapel, echoing its shape and with a large quatrefoil in its gable, seems curiously placed unless it was for the use of the founders of the chapel. Yet another gabled door, the priest's entrance, leads into the chancel on the right.

58 *St Mary Magdalen, Newark, Nottinghamshire: west tower and spire*
59 *St Mary, Ketton, Rutland: view from the south-east*
60 *St Mary, Higham Ferrers, Northamptonshire: view from the west*
61 *St Wulfram, Grantham, Lincolnshire: west tower and spire*

If we had not been familiar all our lives with spires, in image even if not in fact, the array of objects on these two pages would surely seem unbelievably fantastic. What a strange and original notion to build cloud-piercing needles of stone! They are like immensely refined and elongated pyramids and perhaps the comparison is not entirely idle, for there are obvious symbolic affinities.

The rich tower of St Mary Magdalen at Newark, partly Early English, partly Decorated, is crowned by a spire raising its height to 240 feet in one great sweep up to its sky-perched weathercock. The sense of an upward thrust is aided by the sharp triangular broaches at the corners and by the alternating, diminishing dormer-like windows or lucarnes. The delicately crocketed gables of the lucarnes are echoed by those of the bell-openings and upper buttresses. All are in sharp contrast to the plain gables of the buttresses below – for the trellis pattern against which the latter are set marks the top of the Early English work. Its distinctive presence also shows Newark to have been influenced by Lincoln Cathedral. The church owes its surprising grandeur to the fact that although Newark was a continually developing town it could never be divided into separate parishes, because the lord of the manor, who was indeed the Bishop of Lincoln, would not permit it. So civic pride found its outlet in the building of a single magnificent church.

The famous Early English spire of Ketton is the oldest and most austere of the group shown here. From where we are looking nothing disturbs the thirteenth-century image: the chancel lancets lead the eye straight up to the range of tall, slender windows in the tower and the very tall spire, rising directly from the tower with

neither pinnacles nor parapet to conceal the plain broaches.

Higham Ferrers owes its size and opulence to its connection with the house of Lancaster after 1266. About 1325–50 the Early English tower was crowned by an openwork parapet and a crocketed spire which is more attenuated, more recessed than those already considered and joined to its tower by openwork flying buttresses which spring from the corner pinnacles. There are only four lucarnes at each stage, separated by a blank facet of the octagon. The lower tier shows blank tracery in leaf-like Curvilinear forms. The Perpendicular building to the left of the church is the school, re-founded by Archbishop Chichele in 1422.

At Grantham, which reached its astonishing height of over 270 feet in the early fourteenth century, the pinnacles are miniature versions of the spire and hasten its fine ascent. If the pure outline is now beaded by crockets, the lucarnes project so little that they do nothing to interrupt the precipitous slope, while as ornaments they gain by being banded together instead of alternately placed. At the top of the slender broaches are narrow tabernacles containing statues.

62 *St Mary, Clipsham, Rutland: view from the south*
63 *St Mary, Pembridge, Herefordshire: bell-house*

The pyramid form is strongly suggested by the detached bell-house at Pembridge, in the stone-slated lower storey and the roofs of the two weatherboarded upper stages. The structure recalls the timber towers of Essex and the stave churches of Norway, regions where extensive forests influenced building. Sandstone as well as timber was at hand in Herefordshire and the bell-house, built in the late fourteenth century, expresses both materials.

At Clipsham, again in the fourteenth century, the massive pyramid aspires, but it is a rustic version of such noble spires as Ketton. After a first inward slope which almost looks like a false start, the transition from square tower to octagonal spire is made curiously by chamfering the corners. An English peculiarity is the design of the aisle windows, where Curvilinear tracery is confined within a square frame. Clipsham

stone is the hardest of the famous Lincolnshire limestones, and has been much used for
restoration work throughout the country.

*64 St Patrick, Patrington, East Riding of
Yorkshire: view from the south-east*
With its rich flowing tracery and pinnacled
buttresses, Patrington is as overwhelmingly
an image of the fourteenth century as
Ketton is of the thirteenth; but its great spire
(like its large east window) in fact dates
from the Perpendicular period, and thus
forms a fitting close to this sequence. Flying
buttresses scarcely suffice to tether the
needle-sharp, perfectly plain and most
tapering of all these spires to its tower, and
the designer has invented a ravishing cusped
and pinnacled corona of arcading to steady
it.

*65 St Mary, West Walton, Norfolk: south
porch*
*66, 67 St Mary Redcliffe, Bristol: lower stage
of the north porch, and detail of carving on its
outer doorway*
The extraordinary change from the clarity
and repose of thirteenth-century architecture to the flamboyance, movement and
intricacy of the fourteenth-century style
could scarcely be more graphically displayed than by the juxtaposition of these
two porches, separated from each other by
about a hundred years. Polygonal buttresses
flank both doorways, but the diversity of
treatment is so great that the two compositions might belong to different cultures.
An almost classical understatement of
reticent moulding and simple, blank arcading on the one hand contrasts on the other
with the wild romanticism of outward-
leaning ogee canopies crowned by aggressively pointed gables and capricious
outbursts of minutely detailed foliage. This
distinction in buttress design is but the
prelude to the divergence of the sober arch
of the West Walton doorway, enriched by
no more than dogtooth ornament, from the
exotic, utterly idiosyncratic opening at St
Mary Redcliffe, a play upon extravagant
convex and concave curves entirely encrusted with carving reminiscent of Spain
and Portugal and even India – all regions
with which Bristol traded. And indeed the
shape of the door is an exuberant variant on
the multifoil Saracenic arch. In a close-up

view of the carving, of the swelling, deeply
undercut leaves, less well defined than Early
English foliage, but pulsating with a life
which is enhanced by the creatures moving
about among them, birds and beasts, a little
nude man in particular catches the eye.

The porch of St Mary Redcliffe was,
according to William Worcester writing in
1480, 'the principal Chapel of St Mary'. It
contained an altar on the east wall and
several documents mention 'a statue of Our
Lady of the Porch'. Above the stage shown
in the photograph is an upper room where
the church treasures and vestments were
kept (see p. 73).

Though so completely opposed to the
Bristol porch in style, the composition at
West Walton also strikes an unusual if not
altogether alien note. The polygonal pointed caps of the buttresses give the structure a
French or Flemish flavour which the
stepped brick gable reinforces, though this
was a sixteenth-century addition.

*68 St Patrick, Patrington, East Riding of
Yorkshire: interior, looking west from the
south transept*
*69 St Mary, Molland, Devon: interior,
looking east from the south aisle*
Like its great near-contemporary, Holy
Trinity at Hull, the nobly unified church at
Patrington was built from the profits of the
Humber trade. Begun in the late thirteenth
century and completed, except for its spire
(pl. 64), in the early fourteenth century, it
replaced an Early English church, also
cruciform, which had not long been
completed. The shafts of the diamond-
shaped piers press closely to the core, no
longer detached or fully in the round,
the mouldings of capitals and arches are less
dramatically coloured by light and shade
than their Early English predecessors (compare Eaton Bray, pl. 52), and the ornament,
instead of sprouting up and out from the
base of the capital, clings flatly to it, forming
bands of swelling, seaweed-like leaves or of
naturalistic oak, vine and other English
plants. The faces of shafts and arch-
mouldings are enriched by narrow fillets.

Despite its grand scale the Patrington
interior is conspicuous for the absence of
clerestory lights. Although clerestory openings are found in early churches and are used
splendidly at West Walton (pl. 55) and with

great decorative effect at Cley (pl. 71), full use was not made of upper windows until the following century, when they illumined the angel hosts and fine carpentry of great timber roofs (pls. 106, 117, 118).

The piers at Molland, slightly swaying as they raise their blanched arches above the dark oak of the rich eighteenth-century furnishing, reveal a family likeness to those of Patrington, though the shafts are fewer and are separated by angular mouldings. The Molland arcade dates from the last thirty years of the fourteenth century, and this type of pier remained fashionable in Devon throughout the Perpendicular period (see Kenton, pl. 108).

70 St Cuthbert, Great Salkeld, Cumberland: view from the west
Except for its trefoil-headed bell-opening this stark building remains aloof from the ornament which seems so essential to the well-named Decorated style. The sturdy mass of the tower, rendered yet more squat by the huge size of the coarse, irregular sandstone blocks of which it is made and by its skirt of matted ivy, was determined less by fashion than by its geographical position in border country. The Grahams of Netherby and other cattle raiders and marauders were continually harrying the lands of their Cumbrian neighbours, and Great Salkeld had twice been laid waste before this defensive tower was built about 1380. The only entrance to it is from the nave through a strongly barred and iron-plated door. In common with other northern churches dedicated to St Cuthbert, Great Salkeld is said to mark one of the places where the monks of Lindisfarne rested with the relics of the saint when they were driven from Holy Isle by the Danes in 875.

71 St Margaret, Cley-next-the-Sea, Norfolk: south side of the nave
The enchanting design of the nave clerestory, so expressive of the animated Decorated style, is among the distinguishing features of a specially delightful church. A band of cusped cinquefoils alternating with two-light cusped openings runs beneath a fringe of flint-filled arcaded battlements. Circular windows light the clerestories of other churches, but it is only here at Cley and in one other Norfolk

church, Terrington St John, that the motif occurs so strikingly and with this alternating rhythm. The aisles were not finished until the middle of the fifteenth century, which accounts for the character of these south aisle windows with their four-centred arches and with tracery lines which have become rigid and markedly vertical.

72 St Catherine, Ludham, Norfolk: east end
The east window shows the charming variety of Decorated tracery known as 'reticulated'. The complicated effect is simply produced by intersecting diagonal lines that create a net-like pattern in which the openings are cusped. A less intricate example of this form of tracery can be seen in the north transept window at Pembridge (pl. 63).

73 St Mary, Tilty, Essex: east end
The 'chapel by the gate', now the parish church, is all that survives of a former Cistercian abbey, except the wonderfully pastoral setting common to foundations of that Order. The five-light east window, a glorious example of the sinuosity of the developed Curvilinear style, shows exaggerated ogival forms and the mouchette or curved dagger motif in a composition of compelling originality. The flint texture of the wall makes a fine setting for intricate freestone patterns which must have presented grave difficulties to the glazier.

74 St Peter and St Paul, Leominster, Herefordshire: south aisle window
This church was attached to Leominster Priory, but the nave was always used by the parishioners. Robert de Bethune, Bishop of Hereford, consecrated the nave in 1130 and his address to the parishioners has been preserved: 'I pray you all and exhort you by the Lord Jesus Christ, by whose blood ye are redeemed, that ye will think favourably of the Church of St Peter at Leominster; that you will to the utmost of your power entertain friendly and honourable feelings towards the Brethren serving God therein; and will endeavour to support them with your aid, alms and good offices. We know and have learnt by undoubted proofs that the said Church is loved of God.'

Geometric tracery is here, about 1300, undergoing a metamorphosis: the cusped wheel is still present, but it is astir with the suggestion of tremulous flowing patterns, while the heads of the lights are adorned with undulating ribbons within circles; and, the most striking feature of all, these forms and all the mouldings and mullions are overspread with ballflowers.

75 St Mary, Ottery St Mary, Devon: vaults, looking from east to west
Soon after Bishop Grandison of Exeter bought the manor of Ottery St Mary from Rouen Cathedral in 1335 he set about rebuilding the church on an ambitious scale to serve not only the parish but a college of priests. The importance of the building is manifest not just in its size, but in its stone vaults, rare in parish churches, though already seen in the aisles at Patrington (pl. 68). The design of the chancel vault, shown in the foreground of the photograph, magnificently translates the theme of Curvilinear window tracery into a decorative, flowing rib pattern. The sinuous, coiling shapes contrast with the more rigid conventional lierne vault of the crossing and the rib and panel vault of the nave.

76 St Mary Redcliffe, Bristol: vaults of the transepts
This grandiose, cathedral-like church owes its remarkable splendour to the munificence of Bristol merchant princes of the fourteenth and fifteenth centuries, whose wealth came from trade with the Mediterranean and who lived ostentatiously in houses on the river banks. Both record and legend attribute much to the Canynges, the richest of these merchants, the last of whom retired from the world of commerce to become a canon and later the dean of a collegiate church at Westbury-on-Trym.

The great church is vaulted throughout, exhibiting lierne vaults in dazzling variety. This form of vault, so called on account of the use of numbers of purely decorative ribs to connect (in French, *lier*) one point with another, was a fourteenth-century invention, and the south transept vault probably dates from about 1340. The ribs are boldly set out in squares, Maltese crosses, and diamonds, cusped and studded with intricately carved bosses, of which in the whole huge church there are more than a thousand. The boss was not merely orna-

mental: the ends of the ribs fitted into the block of stone upon which it was carved, and thus it locked the vault together.

77 St Margaret, Cley-next-the-Sea, Norfolk: inner doorway of the south porch
The bold curves of the undulating ogee arch, bordered by the shorter more rapid curves of big cusps, and the sweep of the enclosing hoodmould resting on dignified lion-heads state the basic theme of the Decorated style, the flowing linear grace deriving from the fashionable cult of the ogee shape which perhaps itself originated in Saracenic forms seen by crusaders. The doorway is surrounded by an equally ornate Perpendicular porch.

78 St Mary, Thornham Parva, Suffolk: the Crucifixion, central panel of a retable of nine panels
The pathos and assurance of this sophisticated linear picture, reminiscent of contemporary Sienese work with its slender elongated figures set against an undulating background of patterned gold, whets the appetite for further fourteenth-century English masterpieces, but the loss of painting of this kind is almost total. The retable consists of the Crucifixion flanked by eight figures of saints (who include Dominicans). It was only discovered by chance in 1927 when Lord Henniker bought the contents of the home of a Roman Catholic family, Rookery Farm, Stradbroke, at a sale. The sale mark, 'Second Day, Lot 171', still adheres to the back of the panels. The closest surviving parallels are the sedilia paintings in Westminster Abbey, of about 1300, and the retable may indeed be a product of the royal workshops.

79 St Mary the Virgin, Stebbing, Essex: rood-screen
It is an exciting experience to enter the church at Stebbing for the first time. The unpretentious interior is dwarfed and dominated by the rood-screen, which is uncommon in both its material and its design. It is, surprisingly, of stone in a timber region, but its form is still more astonishing: it is not a screen at all in shape but a gargantuan Curvilinear window of three lights, filled with cusped and moulded

flame-like tracery and embellished with
ballflowers. The three plinths on the apexes
of the central ogee arches and rising above
the arcaded transom once supported the
three figures of the Rood – the Virgin and
St John flanking the crucified Christ. The
unconventional character of the screen
perhaps gave rise to criticism, for in the
fifteenth century a normal timber screen
was set up against it. This was removed in
1884 and the stone screen restored. The
history of a similar but rather later stone
traceried screen at Great Bardfield, a few
miles away, is identical.

*80 St Mary, Witney, Oxfordshire:
monuments in the north transept*
The leaping energetic character of Curvilinear tracery is brilliantly realized in the
giant antler-like forms branching from the
heads of the corbel figures leaning out over
the effigies of a nameless man and woman.
These, so flatly recumbent, so unobtrusive,
are almost unremarked under their exotic
cusped and ballflowered ogee arches, which
must have been yet more astonishing when
statues stood on the pedestals in the central
ovals.

81 St Helen, Cliffe, Kent: piscina and sedilia
These seats, terminating at the east end with
a piscina (see the note to pl. 57), all built into
the south wall of the chancel, proclaim their
date, the mid fourteenth century, in the
luxuriance of their vaulted ogee canopies
with towering, budding finials vibrating in
the light from the window behind them.
The celebrant and his assistants sat here
while the Creed and Gloria were being
sung, and the seats are graded in descending
order to correspond to the status of the
officiating priest, the deacon and subdeacon. Later on, when rich endowments
provided many churches with several
clergy in full orders, sedilia were constructed on one level. Above the piscina,
though it is too much in shadow to be seen
in the photograph, is the groove for a shelf
on which the flagons of water and wine
were set out.

82 St Mary, Ottery St Mary, Devon: lectern
In his powerful talons this eagle of gilded
wood clutches an orb on which is the shield
of Bishop Grandison of Exeter. It was he

who donated it to the church in the mid
fourteenth century, so it is one of the earliest
surviving eagle lecterns. Some medieval
lecterns took the form of wooden desks, but
the majority were eagles with outspread
wings, made sometimes of wood but more
often of latten (see the note on pl. 88). As the
emblem of St John the Evangelist, the eagle
was the right choice, for at the beginning of
his Gospel St John takes us into the very
presence of the Divinity like an eagle
soaring up to the sun.

*83 St Mary, Ludgershall, Buckinghamshire:
capital in the nave*
The increased naturalism of fourteenth-
century carving gave rise to an astonishing
variety of expression in sculpture and artists
in different districts developed special styles
of their own. The capitals in a group of
churches on the Oxfordshire-Buckingham-
shire border are carved with crouching
human or grotesque figures instead of
foliage. Among these, this striking capital at
Ludgershall, wreathed with jolly hooded
men leaning forward from under the abacus
with linked arms, is among the most
inventive. The idea occurs again at Hanwell, Oxfordshire, though the design there
is more clumsily organized.

*84 St George, Anstey, Hertfordshire:
misericord*
The chancel stalls in this church, seven of
which are provided with misericords
(brackets placed on the underside of the
hinged seat to give support during the long
standing periods of the medieval service) are
of exceptional interest. For although most
carving of this kind dates from the fifteenth
century, these appear from the church
records to belong to the previous century.
The two men hailing each other with tiny
arms and hands from either side of an oak
spray wear the hood with a point at the back
(also seen on the men on the Ludgershall
capital) which was fashionable from the mid
thirteenth century. The point, known as the
liripip, had grown longer by the fourteenth
century, when hooded headgear assumed
the shape shown in this relief.

*85 Holy Trinity, Long Melford, Suffolk: the
Adoration of the Magi*
Carving in alabaster quarried in Derbyshire

and Staffordshire was the speciality of certain districts, particularly Nottingham, Lincoln and York, in the fourteenth and fifteenth centuries. The most important sculpture in this material was sepulchral (see pl. 128), but a great number of reliefs and small statues were also made and there is evidence of a considerable export trade to the Continent. The reliefs were grouped in wooden frames to form reredoses or retables. The craft was one of the first to reach a commercial level of organization, and late examples display the coarse handling and mannerisms typical of mass production. This Adoration of the Magi in the north aisle at Long Melford, with ox and ass peeping from under the bedclothes, is, however, among the earlier examples, which usually have flat backgrounds and inward-sloping rims. The long shape of this relief indicates that it was probably never part of a retable but was intended for individual exhibition. All such alabasters were originally brightly coloured and gilded, but every trace of paint has vanished from this image, to the advantage of the sensitive modelling and the almost translucent material. Like most other surviving alabaster reliefs, the Adoration is not in its intended position. For long it lay hidden under the chancel floor and only came to light in the eighteenth century.

86 St Lawrence, North Hinksey, Berkshire: font
The fourteenth-century obsession with window tracery declares itself in the ornament of this Decorated font. The panels of the octagonal bowl are carved with reproductions in miniature of the traceried windows of the period.

87 St Giles, Bredon, Worcestershire: coffin-lid
Very few early medieval effigies were actual portraits; but these two early fourteenth-century heads, looming above the arms of the cross, confront us with a piercing look of life. Two holy doves, symbols of the holy spirit, perch on the cross, one for each deceased. The cross itself (usually, according to legend, of wood sprung from the pips of the apple of the Fall) is here made of thorn, the sacred Glastonbury tree, which, with all its offspring, was said to bloom at Christmas.

88 St Mary, Chartham, Kent: brass of Sir Robert de Septvans
Despite religious upheavals and the activities of metal thieves some 10,000 brasses survive in this country, more than in all the other countries of Europe combined. The material of which they are made, much used in the Middle Ages, is latten, an alloy of copper and zinc with a little lead and tin. The earliest examples, like Sir Robert's memorial (1306), are life-size, and all show the same firm, sure draughtsmanship, the lines varying in weight to give expression to the image. This effigy with curling hair like Chaucer's squire – 'lokkes crulle as they were leyd in presse' – is not only a superb linear composition, but a source of minute information about the defensive armour of the period. Sir Robert wears a mail shirt with sleeves ending in mittens (the interlinked iron rings represented by parallel wavy lines). Over the shirt is a linen surcoat, corded at the waist. The sword-belt, sheath and circular pommel are richly decorated and the shield is of the shallow, convex type seen among the Black Prince's achievements at Canterbury. Behind the shoulders are two extraordinary wing-like rectangles, which were indeed known as ailettes. These were fashionable in the fourteenth century and were laced to the sides of the shoulders. Their intention was probably mainly heraldic. Sir Robert's ailettes show his strange device, a winnowing fan (a rebus of his name, Septvans), which reappears with fine decorative effect on his surcoat and shield.

89 Holy Trinity, Ingham, Norfolk: effigy of Sir Oliver de Ingham
This startling figure, eyes open, moving restlessly as though waking from a nightmare induced by his uncomfortable bed of stones, departs from both the contemporary quiet, static type of knightly effigy lying flat with hands clasped in prayer and the more vigorous sword-drawing type of which the Dorchester knight (1310) is the best known example. The strange pebble bed occurs again at nearby Reepham; and the conceit is not altogether surprising in a region where the texture of cottages and farm buildings so often depends on cobblestones from the Norfolk beaches. Sir Oliver died in 1344.

49 St Andrew, Weston, Staffordshire

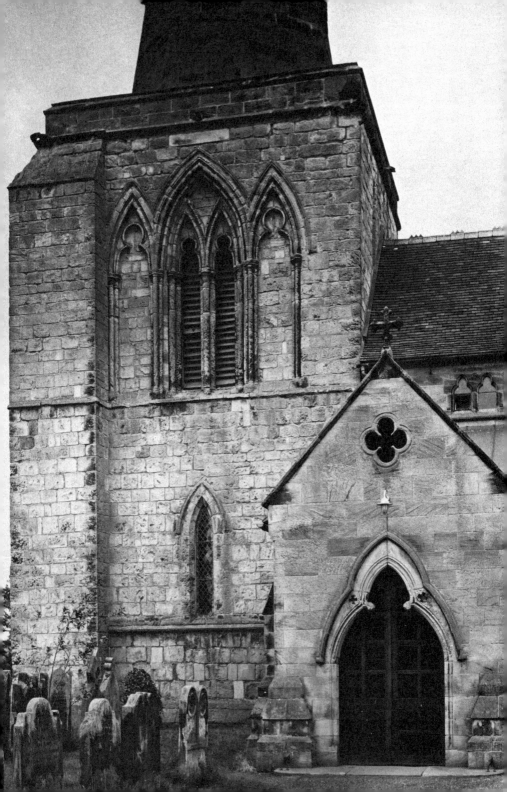

50, 52 *(opposite and right) St Mary, Eaton Bray,
Bedfordshire: south and north aisles*

51 *All Saints, Icklingham, Suffolk:
rush hassocks and chests*

53 *St Leonard, Kirkstead, Lincolnshire*   55 *(opposite) St Mary, West Walton, Norfolk*

54 *St Candida, Whitechurch Canonicorum, Dorset: shrine of St Wite*

56, 57 St Mary, Uffington, Berkshire: view from the south-east, and north transept chapel

58 *(opposite) St Mary Magdalen, Newark, Nottinghamshire*

59 *(left) St Mary, Ketton, Rutland, from the south-east*

60 *(left) St Mary, Higham Ferrers, Northamptonshire*

61 *(above) St Wulfram, Grantham, Lincolnshire*

62 St Mary, Clipsham, Rutland

63 St Mary, Pembridge,
Herefordshire: bell-house

64 (opposite) St Patrick, Patrington,
Yorkshire, from the south-east

65 *St Mary, West Walton, Norfolk: south porch*

66, 67 *(opposite) St Mary Redcliffe, Bristol: lower stage of the north porch, and detail of carving on its outer doorway*

68 *St Patrick, Patrington, Yorkshire, looking west*

70 *(opposite) St Cuthbert, Great Salkeld, Cumberland*

69 *(below) St Mary, Molland, Devon, looking east*

71 *St Margaret, Cley-next-the-Sea, Norfolk*

74 *(opposite) St Peter and St Paul, Leominster, Herefordshire: south aisle windo.*

72 *St Catherine, Ludham, Norfolk: east end*　　73 *St Mary, Tilty, Essex: east end*

75 *St Mary, Ottery St Mary, Devon: chancel (foreground) and nave vaults*

76 *(opposite) St Mary Redcliffe, Bristol: vaults of the transepts*

77 *(opposite) St Margaret, Cley-next-the-Sea, Norfolk: inner doorway of the south porch*

78 *(above) St Mary, Thornham Parva, Suffolk: the Crucifixion, central panel of a retable*

79 (opposite) St Mary the Virgin, Stebbing, Essex: rood-screen

80 (right) St Mary, Witney, Oxfordshire: monuments in the north transept

81 St Helen, Cliffe, Kent: piscina and sedilia

82 (opposite) St Mary, Ottery St Mary, Devon: lectern

83 (above) St Mary, Ludgershall, Buckinghamshire: capital in the nave

84 (below) St George, Anstey, Hertfordshire: misericord

CHAPTER FOUR

From Gothic to Renaissance and Reformation

SCARCELY ANY TWO CENTURIES in English history saw such upheavals and changes as those between Wat Tyler's rebellion in 1381 and the reign of the first Elizabeth; at least not until the Industrial Revolution. The Wars of the Roses filled the first of those two centuries; then after 1485, when Henry Tudor won his throne, came that long century of religious dissension which we know as the Reformation and Puritan movement, eventually culminating in the Civil War.

After the Black Death improvements in agriculture brought bigger yields. The enclosure movement turned many of the older open fields, held in common, into private sheep-runs, obliterating whole villages, depriving many modest owners of commonly cultivated 'furlongs' and turning them into dependent labourers. These, though they might be landless, were free; but their lot worsened. Social and religious dissension grew as wandering friars preached against both lay and religious landlords waxing greater in their estates. Wycliffe's heretical missionaries, with their denial of Transubstantiation in the sacrifice of the Mass, carried new and disturbing ideas to the inhabitants of villages and hamlets. The itinerant preachers stimulated discussion and doubt, which in turn lent growing importance to the sermon as an element in the service; so the pulpit was established *122* as a permanent fixture, one bay west of the chancel arch. Then fixed benches were *119–* introduced into the nave and aisles. An open Bible, now printed in the common *121* tongue of England, was part of Wycliffe's programme; but the unlicensed possession of a printed Bible in English was evidence of heresy until the sixteenth century, when the English Bible and Prayer Book reached all who could read, and many more who could only listen.

The landlords who 'enclosed' made profits. The new town burgesses made profits from trading with the better-off landlords and began to buy land; and yeomen bought smaller, but enclosed, estates. Many of the 'new men' investing in land from trading profits were of knightly families. Such were the Bristol shipping family, benefactors of churches, the Canynges or Cannings; the wool-raisers, weavers and merchants named Spring or Springe of Lavenham, Suffolk; or those named Sylvester of Burford, Oxfordshire. Both the latter built chapels, pews, tombs, even aisles.

Many authorities are puzzled by the great riches which found their way into later Perpendicular churches; whence did they come? The bold and affluent church-building and decorating in this vigorous High Gothic age was financed by profits from newly orientated international trading, new enterprises and improved

117

90 St Andrew, Westhall, Suffolk: south aisle

farming. The stone carvings of merchant ships over the windows outside the Greenway Chapel at Tiverton, Devon, testify to the source of wealth in this region at that period, as do the corbels carved with sheep-shears in the Lane Aisle at Cullompton, Devon. Extra purchasing power not only attracted more luxuries, like spices, as imports in payment for growing exports of wool and cloth, metals, shipping services and fish; it spilled over into beautifying and enlarging existing town and country parish churches, and into building many new churches, or chantry, guild and other subsidiary chapels, and paying the attendant mass-priests' stipends.

The population actually working the newly enlarged landed estates and the older holdings hardly increased. Most of the expansion, following the growing commerce, occurred in the flourishing towns, especially those in the West of England whither the wool trade went from its first base in East Anglia. For with the discovery of the New World the ancient trade routes from the Mediterranean were disrupted and new trade was brought to north-west Europe's seaports facing America. Thus East Anglia's ports and wool centres stagnated and declined, while the newer trade in wool moved westward to Oxfordshire, Gloucestershire, Wiltshire, Dorset, Somerset, and, at last, into Devon and Cornwall, along the belt of stone (see above, p. 18).

It is the more astonishing that so many of the finest Perpendicular churches of England are in what were always small villages (at most seventy householders or taxpayers). It is hard to realize how great was the compulsion, or impulsion, on our forefathers to lay out so much of their modest wherewithal upon their parish church and its contents. Fonts, font-covers, tombs, monuments, screens, effigies, stained glass – all still bear witness, despite the ravages of barbarian zealots, to the high priority accorded by even the most worldly-wise merchants or landlords to the after-life and the powerful mediation of the Holy Church, especially in the local community. One must bear this in mind when visiting the many splendid
106 churches in tiny, sleepy villages: Blythburgh, Bildeston, Stoke by Nayland,
123 Fressingfield, Denston and Dennington in Suffolk; in Norfolk Trunch with its
109 angel roof and staggering two-storeyed font canopy, Ranworth, Salle and Blakeney with its slender beacon tower rising from the chancel; and away to the
94 west Torbryan, Kenton and Bridford in Devon and Launceston and St Winnow in Cornwall, where the carving has been laboriously executed in the local granite.

One-third to one-half of the 10,000 to 11,000 parish churches listed as of architectural or historic importance are either wholly or mainly Perpendicular in style; and they are evenly distributed throughout the land. Edington in Wiltshire shows the appearance of the new style side by side with Decorated forms. The church was built within a decade by Bishop Edington to serve a college for a dean and twelve priests and was finished by 1361. The masons were probably those who had almost certainly inaugurated this peculiarly English style at Gloucester in the 1330s to 1340s. It is emphatically vertical, and richly adorned; in it the Gothic system of screen-wall and buttress reached its inevitable climax as a framework for
106, long ranges of huge windows (memorably exemplified at Blythburgh and
93 Southwold, Suffolk). Instead of the curves of the Decorated style came the right

angle and long runs of straight lines. Instead of wild variety came uniformity. Instead of mystery came clarity. The pointed arch becomes flatter; arches and windows are framed by rectangles. Majestic towers of great height and noble *95–98* proportions make a major contribution to English medieval art. Most of them are square on plan, though octagonal types occur (as at Wickham Market, Suffolk), a few are crowned by an octagonal lantern, as at Fotheringay, Northamptonshire, *91* and a few old East Anglian round towers, like Mutford, Suffolk, were heightened during the fifteenth century by an octagonal belfry stage. Some towers rise in comparative simplicity to a sumptuous parapet, as at Tickhill, Yorkshire; but more *100* frequently their surfaces are covered with tracery and panelling of a predominantly vertical character, as at Boston, Lincolnshire. *95*

Among the many local variations of the style, created in different materials according to the resources of the district, the Somerset stone towers and the East Anglian flint towers call for special mention. The former, which include Huish Episcopi, Mells, Chew Magna, Chewton Mendip, Staple Fitzpaine, St Cuthbert *99* at Wells and St Mary Magdalene at Taunton, fall into categories admirably differentiated by Sir Nikolaus Pevsner in *The Buildings of England: Somerset*. They all display tall pinnacles, an elaborately worked open parapet, pairs of buttresses clasping the corners, a large west window dwarfing the west door and, in the belfry stage, pairs of windows with perforated tracery instead of commonplace louvres. In East Anglia the decoration known as flushwork – a combination of knapped flint and stone producing checkerboard and symbolic patterns along parapets and on buttresses and porches – shows prominently on many towers like those of Eye, Bungay, Lavenham and Monks Eleigh, all in Suffolk. *97*

Interior surfaces of Perpendicular churches are often as richly decorated as those outside: panelling and tracery tend, as in the naves of Lavenham, Suffolk, and Lyddington, Rutland, to fuse the earlier separate units of wall, window and vault. Sometimes, as at Saffron Walden, Essex, the mouldings of the piers are carried *110* straight up to the crown of the arches with no capital, thus merging two distinct structural elements. Worship of straight lines turns even piers and shafts into polygonal rather than rounded members. Carved ornament is less natural, more stylized and stereotyped, the commonest motifs being the Tudor flower and the battlement. Perpendicular vaulting becomes a network of ribs on the surface of the stone unrelated to functional requirements, elaborate reticulation for its own sake; and about 1350 comes the logical outcome of the desire for all-over pattern – the fan vault.

Stone vaults in parish churches of the period are rare, being limited for the most part to porches with upper chambers like those of Cirencester, Gloucestershire, Woolpit, Suffolk, and Dedham, Essex, and to the basements of towers, as at Axbridge, Somerset. The chancel of St Mary's in Warwick is strangely roofed with a composition in which flying ribs seem to support the real ribs on which the vault rests. The church of Ottery St Mary, Devon, is vaulted in every part, while *75* the Lane Aisle at Cullompton in Devon represents the full development of fan *114* vaulting: the spreading fans meet and intersect and the space between the tangents is filled with carved pendants.

One of the great achievements of church builders in the Perpendicular period was the timber roof or ceiling. In Cornwall, Devon and Somerset curved trussed rafters were often boarded on the underside to form a wagon ceiling divided into
115   square panels enriched with carved bosses or tracery, as at Cullompton. In East Anglia the hammerbeam roof became the most striking feature of the parish church. The timber was moulded, crested and gilded, the spandrels displayed openwork decoration, and the hammerbeams (horizontal posts that support the arched braces of the structure, thus reducing the span and allowing the braces to be made of shorter timbers) frequently ended in angels, as at Mildenhall, Suffolk,
117   while heavenly hosts seem to flutter across some roofs, as at March,
118   Cambridgeshire. The amazing two-storeyed hammerbeam roof at Needham Market, Suffolk, is unique.

These intricate roofs were now more illumined by much-enlarged, closely set
93,   clerestory windows like those of Southwold and Blythburgh in Suffolk or
106   Spalding in Lincolnshire. The despoilers of images destroyed most of the stained glass in parish churches; but at Fairford, Gloucestershire, there is a unique run of late fifteenth- to early sixteenth-century windows telling Christian stories and legends, and a considerable proportion of the original glass survives at Wrangle,
134   Lincolnshire, including an almost complete Resurrection. Contemporary dress and other styles are well portrayed in these windows. A stranger example is the little 'Flodden Window' in St Leonard's, Middleton, Manchester, which was mainly rebuilt in 1524 after the battle: Sir Richard Assheton, his wife, chaplain, and leading archers are delightfully shown, the latter with their famous longbows and arrows before going into battle.

The carpenter's art was expressed not only in roofs but also in screens and in the newly introduced benches. The bench-ends were sometimes carved in relief and almost always terminate in finials, or poppy-heads, in the shape of foliage, men or beasts. In the West Country these finials were, however, invariably square-headed and carved with Christian emblems. Surviving benches are so numerous that it is
119–   almost invidious to select examples; but Fressingfield, Blythburgh and Great
121   Bealings in Suffolk, Cley-next-the-Sea and Walpole St Peter in Norfolk, Ivinghoe in Buckinghamshire, Ludlow in Shropshire, and Launcells, St Ives and Goran in Cornwall all show outstanding arrays. Churchwardens' accounts in the fifteenth century reveal that the custom of pew-letting accompanied the institution of fixed seats. At St Michael's in Bath the parishioners paid 7d. each for the year 1441, and in 1520 Hugh Farringdon, Abbot of Reading, paid 4d. for a seat in the church of St Lawrence for his poor and aged mother.

In the fifteenth century the parish church screen reached the luxuriant peak of its development. It displays the same local distinctions as the rest of the church. Rood lofts became general at this time and, like the contemporary minstrels' gallery of the hall house, were designed for musicians, both choristers and instrumentalists, sometimes even for an organist: two organs are recorded to have been made for the rood loft of All Hallows, Barking, in 1519. In general character the wooden screens resemble Perpendicular stonework in their panelling and tracery; but in the West Country, where the screen generally forms the only structural division between nave and chancel, branching fan vaults often spring from the posts to hide the struts or braces supporting the rood loft, the front of which is carved with horizontal bands of foliage as at Kenton, Devon. The wooden screens of Wiltshire, *108* Gloucestershire and Herefordshire are square-panelled, the ceiling under the loft is flat or coved, and the panelled front of the loft is pierced with tracery or adorned with reliefs. The screen of St Margaret's, a tiny isolated church in Herefordshire, *112* shows the delicate, lace-like ornament common in the Welsh border country. East Anglian screens are taller, lighter, and not overshadowed by vaulting and panelling: the loft continues the design as a flat, traceried surface. The screens at Bramfield and around the Bardolph Chapel at Dennington, both in Suffolk, are *111* notable, while that at Ranworth in Norfolk is unusually complete and of a unique *109* design.

A number of East Anglian churches are also remarkable for their fonts. Perpendicular fonts are usually octagonal and set on an octagonal shaft. Both bowl and shaft are panelled and the bowl panels are commonly filled with quatrefoils, quatrefoiled arcading or heraldic devices, as at Ufford, Suffolk; but the new *125* fashion in Norfolk and Suffolk was for figure sculpture representing the Seven Sacraments and the Crucifixion. The fonts at Walsoken and East Dereham in *124* Norfolk are especially well-preserved and arresting examples.

Greater complexity in everyday life and an increasingly secular habit of mind are also reflected in the favoured types of carved effigies and monumental brasses. The latter include not only priests and nobles, but also members of the rising professional and merchant classes. The brasses of Hugh Bostok and his wife (*c.* 1436), of John Heyworth (1520) and his wife at Wheathampstead, Hertfordshire, and of the wool merchant John Browne and his wife in All Saints, Stamford, *132* Lincolnshire, are typical. John Browne wears a purse at his waist and two wool sacks lie at his feet, while his wife flaunts the high waist, turned-down collar, full sleeves and extraordinary horned headdress of the period. Sculptured monuments reveal a new interest in costume and familiarity with foreign fashion. For instance, the magnificent bronze effigy of Richard Beauchamp in his famous chapel in St *127* Mary's at Warwick – not a portrait, despite the strong individuality of the face, for it was not made until fifteen years after the Earl's death in 1439 – reproduces his Milanese armour in minute detail. The use of English alabaster increased after the Black Death. The Bardolph tomb at Dennington, Suffolk, and that of Sir Richard *111* Vernon and his wife at Tong, Shropshire, are executed in this material and show *128* the somewhat angular style. The effigies lie flat on their backs with little variety of pose: they are interesting for the careful rendering of armour and costume. Some alabaster tombs of the first half of the sixteenth century made in the district of Burton on Trent – among them the imposing monument of the Earl of Rutland (d. 1543) at Bottesford, Leicestershire – can be attributed to a known mason-sculptor, Richard Parker. They show signs of the new demand for portraiture in place of the hitherto accepted effigy types. This was symptomatic of the desire of new owners of estates to emphasize their status and to perpetuate their likeness in defiance of the brevity of life. The greater individuality of the sepulchral figure was soon accompanied by a more realistic posture. They now lean on their

elbows in the pose ridiculed by Webster (in *The Duchess of Malfi*, 1623), 'as if they died o' the toothache', like the earlier Fettiplaces at Swinbrook, Oxfordshire, or
130 they kneel, like Grissell Barnardiston at Kedington, Suffolk.

Some of the ostentatious sixteenth-century tombs reflect the revolution in style which had already changed the character of the finest domestic architecture. The tomb of Sir William Cordell at Long Melford, Suffolk, has classical columns
131 supporting coffered arches; the terracotta monuments of Henry (d. 1533) and John (d. 1525), Lords Marney, in Layer Marney Church, Essex, show Renaissance (probably Flemish) influence in both their detail and material. But apart from such tomb details and the occasional use of brick – for the whole church at Layer
101 Marney and for several towers, including those of Sandon, Ingatestone and Rochford, all in Essex – the Renaissance movement had no appreciable effect on parish church architecture until more than a century after the Reformation. For while domestic architecture flourished on the proceeds of the dissolution of the monasteries, parish church-building came to an abrupt halt in the sixteenth century.

Perpendicular as a style has something of ambivalence, of paradox, about it. Possibly every stylistic climax has, since beyond that it is only possible to degenerate. One gets in the finest Perpendicular parish churches of the fifteenth and early sixteenth centuries a sense of impending doom; of strained self-assurance accompanying fear of the hereafter; of propitiation by means of magnificent offerings; of uneasy consciences over newly gained riches; indeed, of the approaching end of the long era of One Belief, One Faith. The imposing screens and roods go up, before going down; the naves and chancels are more grandly screened before being opened up again, and before a new broom sweeps away so much of the older, beautiful work of Englishmen together with their rites and practices. The plain truth is that what the churches were gaining in secular beauty, the Church was losing in spiritual values. The bonds between State and Church were cracking, as those between landlord and tenant, earl and churl, had already cracked.

The Reformation virtually coincided with the 'new learning' of the Renaissance, and the mixture of lay and religious disputes threw all Europe – indeed all Christianity – into convulsions. New nationalistic aims and sentiments arose with the new individualism, emphasizing alike the independence of nations and monarchs and humbler men and women. Old obligations and loyalties were abjured. The 'new man' of the Renaissance, seen in Benvenuto Cellini as artist and Machiavelli as political philosopher, epitomizes the widespread and self-regarding secularism which suddenly pervaded the new outward-looking Western European nations. The most serious schism the Church was ever to suffer was disrupting European societies. It led in England to Henry VIII's dissolution of the monastic and other big land-owning foundations of the Church in 1536 and 1538–39, and his and his courtiers' spoliation and expropriation of their vast properties. He then became head of the Church *of* England, no longer the Church *in* England, claiming that he was a true son of the Catholic Church, but not of the Bishop of Rome. It was not until the reign of Edward VI that notable changes in church services and ritual arrangement took place. They were largely due to the efforts of the anglicized German Martin Bucer, of John Hooper, Bishop of Gloucester, and of Nicholas Ridley, Bishop of London. Ridley and Hooper led a movement to abolish the high stone altars and to set up communion tables instead. Most of the stone altars in the many chantry chapels had already been removed, but high altars now began to be destroyed, roods were torn down (though the screens were often left), Dooms were covered with whitewash, and statues and shrines defaced. This was a prelude to the more terrible iconoclasm in the reign of Charles I of the Puritans, who though active throughout the sixteenth century were kept in check by Elizabeth I's success in imposing a standard religion on her loyal subjects.

A service in the Reformed Church under Elizabeth is not hard to imagine, for in the main the same Prayer Book is still used. The new order of service in English made the churches more community-buildings (their original role); and this must be set against the tragic loss of nearly all medieval stained glass and of most sculpture and painting. Morning and evening prayer were now read in the naves among the people, who in their turn could stand or sit round three sides of the new communion tables in choirs or naves (or, less frequently, in chancels). The table sometimes stood with its short ends facing east and west, sometimes like an altar with its short ends north and south. Prayers were said and the psalms were sung in a rhymed, metrical version to tunes in the psalters. The music was in four parts, 'Cantus', 'Altus', 'Tenor' and 'Bassus', and the singing might be accompanied by viols and wind instruments.

The Royal Arms began to appear prominently in parish churches under Henry VIII, and in 1560 Elizabeth ordered Archbishop Parker to see that 'the tables of the Commandments be comely set or hung up in the east end of the chancel'.

Weekly attendance at church was enforced by the State. The parishioners, as in the past, were summoned to church by bells; but bell-ringing had undergone a transformation. At the Reformation many church bells were either silenced or removed. The task of restoring them under Elizabeth and after necessitated rehanging them, which provided an opportunity to experiment. Most bells were rehung using the whole wheel, while the invention of the slider and the stay made it possible for the bell's movement to be halted at will. After the Reformation the belfry was taken over by the parishioners from the clergy. Extra bells were then installed in many churches and at East Bergholt, Suffolk, where the tower was never completed, a one-storeyed timber bell-cage was built alongside the church with a pyramidal roof, as unique an example of the carpenter's ingenuity as the great roof of Needham Market.   *118*

The upheavals in religious and lay life brought changes in the life of the parish priest. Not more than 200 were deprived of their livings at the Reformation, so there was not much change in the person of the priest. But he had to obey the secular law and became accustomed to altering his religion at the behest of his sovereign, to whom he was now subject. In the small sphere of parish life the squire also now became dominant over the parson. A half affectionate, half contemptuous attitude lies behind Costard's description of the parish priest in *Love's Labour's Lost*: 'a foolish, mild man, an honest man, look you, and soon dashed. He is a marvellous good neighbour, faith; and a very good bowler.' But by the end of Elizabeth I's reign the parson's position was more assured; he was more certain of his message, more respected. Under Elizabeth the clergy, forbidden to marry in Queen Mary's reign, were again authorized, this time for good, to take wives. The scene was thus set for the rearing of a notable race of children in the parsonages of England for many generations to come.

Notes on the plates

90 St Andrew, Westhall, Suffolk: south aisle
This atmospheric photograph suitably introduces the Perpendicular theme: light streams in through a window with a four-centred arch filled with simple rectilinear tracery, in which the main mullions run straight through from sill to arch; and the shadowy benches, though most of them are Victorian copies of the few fifteenth-century survivals, vividly evoke the period when the sermon first became an important element in the service and pews, instead of being a rare luxury, were provided for the whole congregation.

91 St Mary and All Saints, Fotheringay, Northamptonshire: view from the north-east
This buoyant image, unlike most parish churches, which belong to different periods, is all of a piece, for it was completely rebuilt when Edmund Plantagenet decided to found a college at Fotheringay. The chancel was demolished after the Dissolution but the surviving nave with its flying buttresses and double range of huge windows is of special interest because we know the name of the designer. He was the master mason William Horwood, and the contract of 22 September 1434 between him and 'Will Wolston Sqwier and Thomas Pecham clerke, commisaris for the hy and mighty prince and my right redouthed lord, the duc of Yorke' (Edmund's great-nephew) has been preserved. One of the most enchanting of Perpendicular conceits is the setting of an octagonal storey on a square tower. Examples include All Saints Pavement, York, and the Boston Stump (pl. 95). The elegant Fotheringay lantern, the shape of which is engagingly repeated in miniature in the corner turrets, served as a beacon to guide travellers through the extensive and dangerous forest of Rockingham.

92 St Nicholas, Bromham, Wiltshire: south chapel

93 St Edmund, Southwold, Suffolk: south side of the nave
94 St Mary Magdalene, Launceston, Cornwall: view from the east
The characteristic Perpendicular design of screen walls and buttresses with enormous windows stretching from one buttress to the next achieved splendour and richness in a variety of ways depending on the locality of the church and the materials available. The elaborate ornament of the late fifteenth-century Tocotes and Beauchamp Chapel at Bromham, the wiry precision of the tracery, the delicate carving of the angels on the apexes of the windows and of the bull-gargoyle, the ornate buttresses and pinnacles, the sumptuous frieze of foliage and quatrefoil patterns, the moulded battlements displaying heraldic devices and superimposed on quatrefoils, all owe their striking and exquisite finish to the quality of the fine oolitic limestone found in this corner of Wiltshire.

At Southwold, built about 1430–60, the dark and sparkling wall of local dressed flint provides a brilliant foil to the glitter of glass and to the imported stone of mullions, mouldings and parapet, while flint and stone combine to produce the bold checkerwork of the buttresses.

The frenzied, barbarous aspect of the amazing ornamentation at Launceston is largely due to the intractable granite in which it has all been painstakingly carved – coarse heraldic beasts, urns and finials and the contrasting lace-like surface decoration of fleurs-de-lis, quatrefoils, coats of arms, palm leaves, roses, thistles, pomegranates and canopied niches. Under the central of the three east end windows (terminating the chancel and the aisles which, in a style peculiar to Cornwall and Devon, run from west to east without any break in height) lies the vigorous figure of the saint to whom the church, built in 1511–24 by Sir Henry Trecarrel, is dedicated.

*95 St Botolph, Boston, Lincolnshire: view
from the south
96 Holy Cross, Great Ponton, Lincolnshire:
view from the west
97 St Peter and St Paul, Lavenham, Suffolk:
view from the west
98 St James, Chipping Campden,
Gloucestershire: view from the south-west*
Among all the buildings which have
enriched the English landscape, Perpendicular towers are conspicuous for a
staggering variety of design which is not
just due to the styles of local schools of
craftsmen working in many different
materials, but which expresses an overwhelming imaginative force.

Boston, Lavenham, Great Ponton and
Chipping Campden all owe their
magnificence to merchants as enthusiastic
for self-advertisement as for the glory of
God. Boston was built chiefly in the reign of
Edward III to cater for the inhabitants of a
rapidly growing trading centre: the giant
building seated nearly 3,000 people. The
glorious tower, however, is wholly Perpendicular though of three different periods
– first, the panelled stages ending above the
pair of two-light windows, then the stage
with the vast uncusped four-light window,
and finally the octagonal lantern at the top.
Part of the cost was borne by 'merchauntes
of the Stilard' or Steelyard, where the
Hanseatic League was established. The
ornate, silvery tower of Great Ponton
proclaims the wealth and importance of
Anthony Ellis, a wool stapler of Calais, as
well as gratitude for his safe return to
Lincolnshire (with his chests of gold). His
coat of arms shows prominently on the west
face of the tower.

The church at Chipping Campden, given
its present magnificent form after 1450,
with the proceeds of the wool trade,
contains the tomb of William Grevel,
described on his brass as 'the flower of the
wool merchants of the whole realm of
England'. St Peter and St Paul at Lavenham
was financed by local clothiers, the Springs,
and by the lord of the manor, John de Vere,
whose families were eventually united by
marriage. The tower was built between
1486 and 1525 and is encrusted with
reminders of both the de Veres and the
Springs, especially the latter. Their merchant marks share the flushwork decoration

of the base with the keys of St Peter and the
swords of St Paul, while the recently
acquired coat of arms of the third Thomas
Spring appears no less than thirty-two times
on the parapet. The stone stars shining
against the dark knapped flint of the
masonry do not, as might be thought,
represent constellations in the night sky but
commemorate the de Veres, who took the
star as their emblem.

Each of these churches is sited where its
architectural character is most splendidly
effective. The 272 feet of Boston's slender
panelled tower shoot up from the quay by
the Witham, exaggerated by reflections, to
dominate the surrounding fenland, a landmark from as far away as the other side of
the Wash. In the Middle Ages its octagonal
lantern guided wayfarers over the trackless
morass and signalled to mariners crossing
the Lynn Deep. The Lavenham tower
commands the landscape from a great
distance to the west and looks its best when
struck by sunset light, which sets the indigo
hearts of its knapped flints afire, concentrates attention on its mass and brings
out the detail and dramatic chiaroscuro of its
highly individual buttresses. Great Ponton,
heavier and less aspiring, reveals the rich,
immaculate detail of its carved ornament
and of buttresses as unusual as those of
Lavenham (for they suddenly change from
square to polygonal shapes in the huge bell
stage) only at close quarters, in a more
intimate, wooded setting. Chipping Campden forms the stately climax to a serene
Cotswold village.

*99 St Andrew, Mells, Somerset: tower, seen
from the east*
At Chipping Campden (pl. 98) the panelling, which is such a conspicuous feature of
the Perpendicular style, invades the traceried window spaces, leaving only four lights
open at the belfry stage. The early sixteenth-
century tower at Mells shows a typical
Somerset variant of this arrangement:
pierced tracery in the shape of tiny
quatrefoils takes the place of the usual
louvre-boards in the bell stage, which
otherwise exactly mirrors the design of the
stage below it. A rich, inventive play upon
diagonally set pinnacles gives the tower
sparkle and movement.

100 St Mary, Tickhill, West Riding of Yorkshire: view from the south-west
The fretted, fringe-like pattern of the parapet created by setting crocket-encrusted pointed arches between the battlements is a Yorkshire feature seen again at Beeford, Thirsk, Holme and Holy Trinity at Hull. The rich airy bell stage, and the storey below it with its frieze, its gabled buttresses and its niches still containing their original statues, is an altogether lighter structure than the lower stage with its massive buttresses. The upper part belongs to the period when Tickhill, originally a thirteenth-century church, was taking on its present basically Perpendicular aspect. It was still being altered in 1429 when a parishioner, John Sandford, made a bequest of a cart and four horses 'to the makyng of the stepall'.

101 St Andrew, Sandon, Essex: tower and south porch
In the early sixteenth century brick, which had scarcely been used as a main constructive material since the departure of the Romans from Britain, became extremely fashionable. At Sandon a tower and porch of red brick add rich colour to an earlier building of local flint and septaria. The notion of patterning the fabric with purple bricks originated in France. The X shapes at Sandon both symbolize the patron saint – crucified on a saltire cross – and represent the primatial cross of Cardinal Wolsey, lord of the manor, who was involved with the building of the tower and porch.

102 St Mary, Woodbridge, Suffolk: north porch
This exotic building, mentioned in a bequest of 1455, presents one of the most extreme displays of the peculiarly East Anglian technique of flushwork, already glimpsed at Southwold (pl. 93) and Lavenham (pl. 97). The typical Perpendicular panel decoration is here carried out in knapped flint and cut stone, so that a flat black-and-white pattern takes the place of relief ornament. This use of materials is found nowhere outside England. The devices on this porch include the crowned M of Our Lady, the monogram of the Holy Trinity, the chalice and Host and a miniature Perpendicular window.

103 St Peter and St Paul, Northleach, Gloucestershire: south porch
Of the two-storeyed porches, first introduced in the fourteenth century but commoner in the fifteenth, this is one of the most finely detailed and harmonious. The central two-tiered niche placed between traceried panels and merged with the ogee hoodmould of the door is the essential unifying feature. The existence of a fireplace, an oven and candle-sconces in the porch chamber suggests that the room was meant for habitation, probably by the priest. The chimney flue is cleverly concealed in a buttress on the west wall. The exceptionally fine workmanship is associated with the name of a rich benefactor, the wool merchant Fortey.

104 St Mary the Virgin, Saffron Walden, Essex: south porch
By comparison with the three other porches shown here this late fifteenth-century design, carried out in clunch and flint rubble and imported stone, is nobly reticent. It is distinguished by buttresses which imitate the polygonal stair turret. The upper chamber was once used for a school maintained by the Guild of the Holy Trinity, incorporated by Henry VIII in 1513. The schoolmaster was the Guild priest, who also sang masses for the souls of departed members in the Chapel of the Trinity.

105 St John the Baptist, Cirencester, Gloucestershire: south porch
The porch was added to the church in about 1490. It looks almost transparent with its huge oriels, hollowed niches, openwork pinnacles and filigree battlements. The porch is secular in appearance and its purpose was secular, for it served as an office for the discussion of financial matters between the Royal Commissioners and the neighbouring abbot who owned the manor and held a monopoly of the wool. One of the two upper storeys was used for the meetings of trade guilds. After the Dissolution the porch became the town hall. It only reverted to the vicar in the eighteenth century.

106 Holy Trinity, Blythburgh, Suffolk: interior, looking west
The tranquillity and regularity of this

spacious, luminous interior, the quiet rhythm of the quatrefoil piers and simply moulded arches and the contrasting movement of the big, deeply set clerestory windows, are emphasized by the whitewash which replaces the original wall-paintings. And the white walls find an echo in the white elements of the almost flat tie-beam roof, where great primitive angels unfold their wings against a background of partly painted, partly stencilled flowers, sacred emblems and monograms. The angels look down on the matrices of the stolen brasses of benefactors of the church and bear the shields of the lords of the manor, the Hoptons and their connections, who helped to finance the rebuilding of Holy Trinity in the mid fifteenth century. Of the earlier church the only survival is the west tower, severely plain apart from the exquisite Decorated window seen in the distance beyond the typical East Anglian font.

107 St Andrew, Lyddington, Rutland: interior, looking north-east
If Blythburgh depends for its effect upon light and space, here it is the upward surge of the slender piers which most strikes the spectator. The design of these piers is similar to those of the Suffolk church but here the shafts alternate with hollow mouldings in a design typical of the period, and the polygonal capitals are so insignificant that they encourage rather than interrupt the soaring movement of the arcades. The photograph shows the characteristically tall bases of Perpendicular piers, with mouldings like the pinched-out clay of a pot lid oversailing the foot.

108 All Saints, Kenton, Devon: rood-screen
Many of the Perpendicular churches of Devon and Cornwall were planned with aisled chancels, like Launceston (pl. 94), and thus, as there was no structural division between nave and chancel, the rood-screen was carried right across the building. The sumptuous Kenton screen is also expressive of its locality in the details of its design. The traceried openings above the painted wainscot base take the form of Perpendicular windows and above them rises a rood loft, the supports of which are concealed by fans. The bressumer, in common with many another, appropriately displays a flowing vine motif (alluding to Christ the True Vine, and to the wine of the Eucharist), deeply cut on a scale which draws attention to the rich, minute detail of the canopied angels and the fretted cresting above them. The screen, well restored at the beginning of the present century, was originally, in about 1480, the combined work of local and Flemish carvers.

109 St Helen, Ranworth, Norfolk: screen
This exceptionally pretty structure is of special interest because of its unique design, with taper holders joined by crocketed flying buttresses to partition walls dividing little side altars from the actual rood-screen. Though lighter in character and on a more intimate scale it is similar in type to the Kenton example (pl. 108), with its fan coving and window-like openings, and is recognizably East Anglian only in the style of the gentle, linear paintings of saints and angels in the panels. Their counterparts are to be found at Southwold, Tunstead and Ludham. There is also a distinct suggestion of immediate locality in the enchanting incidental painted decorations which include the marsh buttercup, the yellow iris and the waterfowl of the surrounding Broadland. Beyond the screen is a Laudian communion rail (see p. 161).

110 St Mary the Virgin, Saffron Walden, Essex: nave seen from the chancel
The arcades of this grand interior are even taller than those at Lyddington and their height is exaggerated by the unbroken sweep of the outer moulding of the arches and lozenge-shaped piers, and by shafts towards the nave which shoot up above the arches to reach the clerestory. The remarkable unity of the design is enhanced by the repeated Tudor rose ornament in the spandrels, and the effect of height gains from the change in material from stone to the brilliantly white local clunch of the clerestory. The design of the nave was traditionally attributed to John Wastell, who was working on King's College Chapel, Cambridge, from 1508, and a contract of 1485 discovered some twenty-five years ago at Cambridge corroborated the tradition. The coat of arms of the tower wall is that of Charles II.

111 St Mary, Dennington, Suffolk: screen of the Bardolph Chapel
Chantry chapels proliferated in the Perpendicular period. Here the alabaster effigies of Lord and Lady Bardolph (1441) are enclosed by a traceried screen of the type most commonly found in East Anglia. It is much less massive than the Kenton screen (pl. 108), and more austerely rectilinear. Above the solid wainscot base delicate tracery and crocketed ogee arches adorn open rectangular panels and, above them, the loft, which scarcely projects beyond the screen.

112 St Margaret, south-west Herefordshire: rood-screen
A type of conspicuously rectangular design remarkable for the profusion of minutely carved ornament found only in the Welsh Marches and in Wales itself is represented by this masterpiece of meticulous carving, installed about 1520 in a tiny church now far from any village. It combines pattern and poetry with the most vivid, graphic rendering of plant forms. The rood loft here has become a wide gallery resting on carved posts. The text with its border is an interesting survival of post-Reformation decoration and specifically of that enjoined by Canon LXXXII of 1604, which stated that texts were to correspond to the function of each part of the church: this sentence from *Isaiah* is painted next to the pulpit.

113 St Lawrence, Clyst St Lawrence, Devon: rood-screen
114 St Andrew, Cullompton, Devon: vaulting of the Lane Aisle
The fact that the tracery has gone from the arches of the Clyst St Lawrence screen concentrates the eye on the close resemblances of the two palmate growths, one carried out in wood, the other in stone. And indeed, in construction and design, as the examples on the previous pages show, timber screens were largely based on stone forms.
The Lane Aisle was built in about 1525 by a wool merchant, John Lane, whose tomb slab, shorn of its brass effigy, lies below the spreading fans. Fan vaulting is in a way the apotheosis of the Gothic period in England, a purely English development, invented at

Gloucester Cathedral. One of its charms is that it is equally satisfying whether branching in miniature over a porch or a tomb or expanding to cover the roof of a great college chapel or cathedral choir. The Lane Aisle vault, carried out in local Beer stone, is of the same type as the most glorious fan ceiling of all, in the Henry VII Chapel at Westminster Abbey, where the fans intersect. The angel corbels from which the fans spring are carved with instruments of the Passion and with John Lane's sheep-shears, and a fleece with two crossed spears.

115 St Andrew, Cullompton, Devon: nave ceiling
116 St Mary, Stamford, Lincolnshire: ceiling decorated the north chapel
The wagon vaults of the West Country were often plastered and whitewashed, but occasionally they were boarded and decorated with the panelled richness characteristic of the woodwork of the region, as here at Cullompton, where the crested diagonal ribs, bosses and angels, all brilliantly lit by large clerestory windows, still show much the same gilding and colouring as blazed from them in the Middle Ages.
The panelled ceiling of what was once the Chapel of the Corpus Christi Guild in St Mary, Stamford is a flatter, simpler version of the same type of structure. It was given by William Hikham and his wife and the family resemblance between some of the boss heads suggests that they may be likenesses of the donors and their connections.

117 St Wendreda, March, Cambridgeshire: nave roof
This double hammerbeam roof (see p. 120), constructed about 1500, shows a totally different form of timber construction, one which, like the fan vault, belongs essentially to the Perpendicular period. The open structure leads the eye upwards to where, higher, more than a hundred angels seem to be just alighting on the wall posts, on the finely carved cornice, on the hammerbeams and on the braces, filling the air with the rush of their pinions.

118 St John the Baptist, Needham Market, Suffolk: nave roof
At March (pl. 117) it is the host of moth-like

angels which stirs the imagination: at Needham Market it is the actual stupendous construction which is unforgettable. The design echoes that of the church below: it is an aerial nave borne up by the wings of the hammerbeam angels. The tall posts rising from the hammerbeams to the full height of the roof are like arcade piers and vaulting shafts and above them, as in any grounded nave, the structure is lit by clerestory windows, two-light and trefoil-headed. The building of the church – otherwise unremarkable – was paid for by Bishop Grey, Bishop of Ely from 1458 to 1478.

119 St Peter and St Paul, Fressingfield, Suffolk: benches
120 St Margaret, Cley-next-the-Sea, Norfolk: poppy-head
121 St Mary, Ivinghoe, Buckinghamshire: poppy-head
The earliest pews in English churches (pp. 117, 120) belong to the great age of English woodwork. Sometimes, as at Fressingfield, the whole of the bench-end is overlaid with traceried panels. The poppy-heads in which these ends terminate take the common form of trefoiled foliage; they sometimes show the figures of men and beasts, but more often than not the two are merged in images which bring us into sharp, strange contact with a world where the terror of the cornfield and the dark forest was a living force. The man who wrought those vital leaves at Fressingfield felt they were animated by more than vegetable power, a power which takes tangible form in the bulging inhuman eyes, the ferny lips and leaf hands of the Cley carving and in the monumental composition at Ivinghoe. They embody beliefs and rites older than Christianity. The ancient spring sacrifice of the Grass King, represented by a man covered with a cage and mask of greenery, is commemorated by the creature at Cley, while at Ivinghoe we encounter the likeness of the bogle, who was nothing but an earth-brown face with staring eyes looking from a tangle of hair and grass on the edge of cornfields or in haunted spinneys.

122 St Mary and All Saints, Fotheringay, Northamptonshire: pulpit
The pulpit was only established as a permanent part of the church furniture after the Reformation. It seems previously to have been a movable structure. The Fotheringay pulpit, of the early sixteenth century, delicately carved with Perpendicular ornament and with a delightful little ribbed vault with pendants under the later Jacobean tester, is still attached in its original position, to the pier on the north side of the chancel arch.

123 St Botolph, Trunch, Norfolk: canopy over the font
This extraordinary object, one of the countless surprises awaiting the parish church enthusiast, so entirely dominates the aisleless interior that it is many minutes before the dazzled eye can appreciate the restraint of the fine hammerbeam roof above it. Instead of resting on the font, the theatrical cover rises in the form of a canopy from six enclosing piers as profusely carved as the shafts of the amazing pulpit at Kenton (pl. 108). The exotic superstructure is like a giant crown formed of ogee niches, each with its own miniature fan vault, surmounted by jostling battlemented castles and crowned by an openwork, leaf-sprouting ogee cupola. Figure paintings of New Testament subjects once filled the niches, and flying buttresses connecting the canopies to the pillars accelerated the sense of bursting, swelling movement. When the colours and gilding were fresh the composition must have looked almost garish. Now the remnants of faded gold, pink, ochre and dark green on the ashen wood inform the whole robust image with unexpected, nostalgic poetry.

124 All Saints, Walsoken, Norfolk: font
This is one of the best preserved of the more than thirty examples of Seven Sacraments fonts in Norfolk and Suffolk (see p. 121). The photograph shows the scenes of the Crucifixion and Extreme Unction. Round the base are carved the instruments of the Passion and an inscription recording John Bedford, Chaplain, and S. Honiter and his wife, with the date 1544. The flowering ogee niches with their little vaults echo those of the Trunch canopy (pl. 123).

125 St Mary, Ufford, Suffolk: font
The tiered font cover, eighteen feet tall and reaching like a bedizened spire to the tie-

beam of the roof, is as spectacular as the Trunch canopy and with its elongated, spiky, crocketed, fretted, extraordinarily delicate forms and finials, a complete contrast to it in feeling as well as shape. The Gothic spirit is still strong at Ufford. The cover is furnished with a remarkable telescopic device enabling the base and lowest tier to be pushed up for the baptismal ceremony without raising the whole structure. William Dowsing, the Cromwellian iconoclast, was scandalized by this wonderful contrivance, 'like a pope's triple crown, with a pelican on top picking its breast, all gilt over with gold'. But except for wrenching the images of the saints from the niches, he let it stand.

126 Holy Trinity, Stratford on Avon, Warwickshire: chancel
This chancel, built by Dean Balshall (whose carved tomb chest can be seen on the left in the photograph) at the end of the fifteenth century, well illustrates the splendour and unity of the fully developed Perpendicular interior. The building itself is simple — a broad rectangular space walled with panelled glass. But a rich encrustation of ornament gives life and warmth to the 'functional' framework. Though the original glass has been replaced by Victorian work, the effect of the brilliant translucent colours in the tracery and tall cusped lights specially designed for the framing of glass paintings can still be felt. And the sense of opulence is encouraged by the ornate roof, by the panels between the windows, the elaborate door and the saints on either side of the east window, standing in niches which burst into growth above the figures and appear to be carried upwards on the wings of the curious giant dragonflies forming the brackets. Shakespeare lies buried in this chancel, just below his wall monument by Gerard Johnson on the far side of the door at the left.

127 St Mary, Warwick: Beauchamp Chapel
This, the most sensational of chantry chapels in parish churches, has the same air of private, aristocratic luxury as the saloon with its blue quilted ceiling in Queen Victoria's railway carriage and is of much the same proportions. The charming fan vault has only three fans on each side. The

chapel is one of the best documented of medieval buildings. It was begun in 1443 under the will of Richard Beauchamp, Earl of Warwick, completed in 1464 and consecrated in 1475. It cost £2148 4s. 7½d. There was originally a fifteenth-century Doom painting above the balconied entrance, but this was combined with a copy of Michelangelo's *Last Judgment* by Richard Bird in 1678.

128 St Bartholomew, Tong, Shropshire: tomb of Sir Richard and Lady Margaret Vernon
Sir Richard Vernon died in 1451, when alabaster tomb chests and effigies had been fashionable for about seventy years. His fine monument in the Golden Chapel, named after its once gilded fan vault, follows the style established by the alabaster shops in the last quarter of the fourteenth century (see above, note to pl. 85). The sides of the chest are decorated with canopied niches divided by miniature buttresses and in them stand 'weepers', which might be relatives but which here take the form of saints and angels. Lady Margaret's dress was fashionable at the time of her death. She wears a long cloak fastened with richly carved brooches and her hair is confined in a jewelled net or 'crespine' bunched over the ears in 'cauls' joined by an embroidered band.

129 St Mary the Virgin, Layer Marney, Essex: tombs of Sir William Marney and Henry, Lord Marney
Sir William Marney's effigy, seen in the background, is another example of the alabaster sepulchral sculpture of which so much survives from the two centuries following the Black Death. The figure displays interesting costume details: he wears a pointed bascinet with the 'camail' or curtain of mail hanging from it to protect the neck, and the jupon with a sword-belt low on the hips, all fashionable in the early fifteenth century. Sir William's tomb is enclosed by its original carved oaken posts.

The black marble likeness of Henry, Lord Marney, who died in 1523, exhibits the fashion details of a century later. The style of his bobbed hair and blunt-toed shoes belongs to the time of his death. But it is the elaborate four-poster on which Lord Marney is stretched which draws the eye.

Wholly Renaissance in character, it is made of a material unknown in the Middle Ages — terracotta, that finer counterpart of brick introduced into England by Italian craftsmen in the reign of Henry VIII. This balustered canopy is no doubt by the same hand as the terracotta motifs which distinguish the fantastic gatehouse of Lord Marney's unfinished mansion, Layer Marney Towers.

130 St Bartholomew, Quorndon, Leicestershire: detail from the monument of John Farnham
Reliefs behind the recumbent effigy of John Farnham (d. 1587) show him in full active life on the battlefield. This is more than a record of the dead man's achievements: it is an affirmation in the face of death of life itself and the enduring consequence of the deceased, a typical Elizabethan product. The tomb is attributed to the outstanding Elizabethan sculptor Epiphanius Evesham.

131 St Peter and St Paul, Kedington, Suffolk: effigy of Grissell Barnardiston
In a church crammed with fascinating objects the fierce, concentrated energy of this compact, formidable figure compels instant attention. Coloured with the hues of life, open-eyed, fashionably dressed, alertly kneeling instead of lying in the sleep of death, she testifies to the secular bias of her age. Grissell was a spinster who died in 1609.

132 All Saints, Stamford, Lincolnshire: brasses of John and Margery Browne
Brasses of civilians of the merchant and legal classes only occur after the end of the fourteenth century. John Browne, a wool stapler, died in 1442, his wife in 1460. Both wear the loose, baggy garments drawn in at the waist and the bishop's sleeves fashionable in the mid fifteenth century. A purse hangs at John Browne's belt; his hair is cut short and he is clean-shaven except for a tuft of hair on the chin, a fashion which went out some twenty years before the wearer's death. Margery Browne's heart-shaped headdress was contrived with the aid of a wire framework and is as typical of her time as her turned-down collar. The quality of the line in these brasses is less striking than

that of brasses of the previous century (see pl. 88), for its purity has been marred by the mistaken introduction of hatched lines to give the semblance of a third dimension to the figures.

133 St Mary and St Nicholas, Wrangle, Lincolnshire: the Resurrection, detail of the east window
An inscription formerly part of this splendid window is recorded to have stated that it was made to the order of Thomas de Wynesty, Abbot of Waltham from 1345 to 1371. A late medieval date for the glass is indicated by the naturalism of the figures, the type of armour worn by the soldiers (camail, bascinet and sallet, which replaced the bascinet), the predominance of canopy work, by the fact that the mosaic technique of early glass painting has been abandoned for larger areas of colour and above all by the use of silver nitrate (a late fourteenth-century discovery) to produce a magical range of yellow tints ranging from palest lemon to rich amber.

134 St Bartholomew, Quorndon, Leicestershire: tomb-slab of Thomas Farnham and his wife
Among the remarkable monuments in the Farnham Chapel at Quorndon (see also pl. 129) are several incised slabs standing upright against the wall that date from about 1500. The technique in which these charmingly naive linear images have been executed is unique in England; it is of Italian origin and can be seen at its best in the cathedral in Siena. Thomas Farnham, who died in 1500, wears the armour of his period with prominent shoulder guards and mail skirt with jointed plates of steel, while Margaret Farnham wears widow's weeds.

135 St Dunstan, Cranbrook, Kent: south door
We take our leave of the medieval church through an oaken door which is a complete fifteenth-century survival. By the time this door was made the smith had little opportunity to exhibit his former artistry (see pls. 37 and 50), and the linear reinforcement is simply applied by means of glue and nails. The churchwardens provided the timber and paid 17s. 7d. for the work.

91 St Mary and All Saints, Fotheringay, Northamptonshire, from the north-east

92 St Nicholas, Bromham, Wiltshire: south chapel

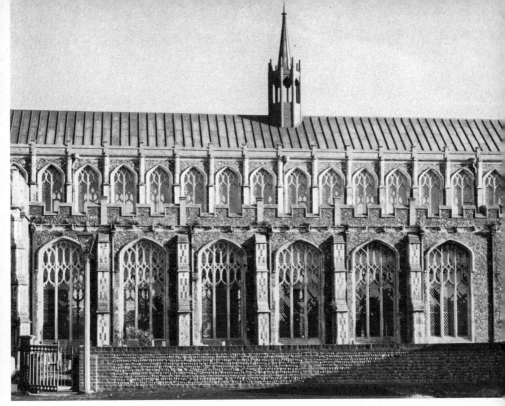

93 *St Edmund, Southwold, Suffolk: south side of the nave*

94 *St Mary Magdalene, Launceston, Cornwall, from the east*

95 (opposite) St Botolph, Boston, Lincolnshire

96 (above) Holy Cross, Great Ponton, Lincolnshire

97 St Peter and St Paul, Lavenham, Suffolk

98 (below) St James, Chipping Campden, Gloucestershire

99 (opposite) St Andrew, Mells, Somerset: the tower, seen from the east

100 St Mary, Tickhill, Yorkshire: view from the south-west

101 St Andrew, Sandon, Essex: tower and south porch

102 (left) *St Mary, Woodbridge, Suffolk: north porch*

103 (below) *St Peter and St Paul, Northleach, Gloucestershire: south porch*

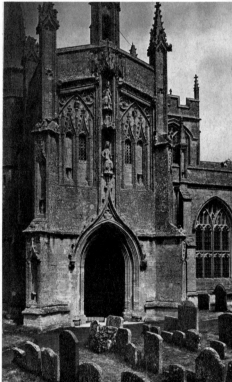

104 (left) *St Mary the Virgin, Saffron Walden, Essex: south porch*

105 (opposite) *St John the Baptist, Cirencester, Gloucestershire: south porch*

06 (opposite) Holy Trinity, Blythburgh, Suffolk, looking west

07 (above) St Andrew, Lyddington, Rutland, looking north-east

108 *All Saints, Kenton, Devon: rood-screen*

109 *(below) St Helen, Ranworth, Norfolk: screen*

110 *(opposite) St Mary the Virgin, Saffron Walden, Essex: the nave seen from the chancel*

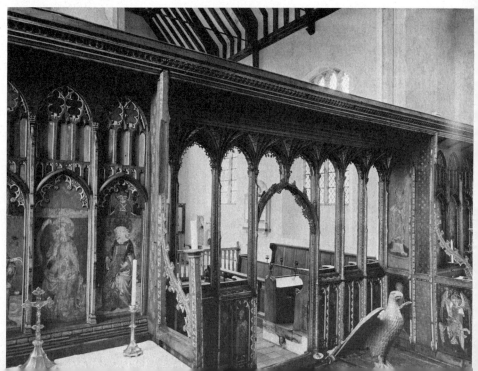

111 (left) St Mary, Dennington, Suffolk:
screen of the Bardolph Chapel

112 (below) St Margaret, south-west
Herefordshire: rood-screen

113 (left) St Lawrence, Clyst St Lawrence,
Devon: rood-screen

114 (opposite) St Andrew, Cullompton, Devon:
vaulting of the Lane Aisle

115 St Andrew,
Cullompton, Devon:
ceiling of the nave

116 (right) St Mary,
Stamford, Lincolnshire:
ceiling of the north chapel

117 (opposite) St
Wendreda, March,
Cambridgeshire: nave roof

118 (opposite) St John the Baptist, Needham Market, Suffolk: nave roof

119 (below) St Peter and St Paul, Fressingfield, Suffolk: benches

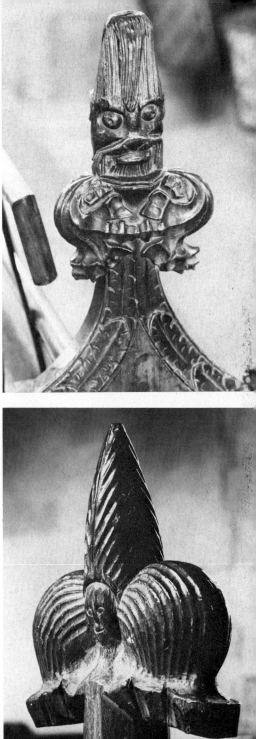

120 (above right) St Margaret, Cley-next-the-Sea, Norfolk: poppy-head

121 (right) St Mary, Ivinghoe, Buckinghamshire: poppy-head

122 (below) St Mary and All Saints,
Fotheringay, Northamptonshire: pulpit

123 (right) St Botolph, Trunch, Norfolk:
canopy over the font

124 (right) All Saints, Walsoken, Norfolk: font

125 (opposite) St Mary, Ufford, Suffolk: font

126 *Holy Trinity, Stratford on Avon, Warwickshire: chancel*

127 *(opposite) St Mary, Warwick: Beauchamp Chapel*

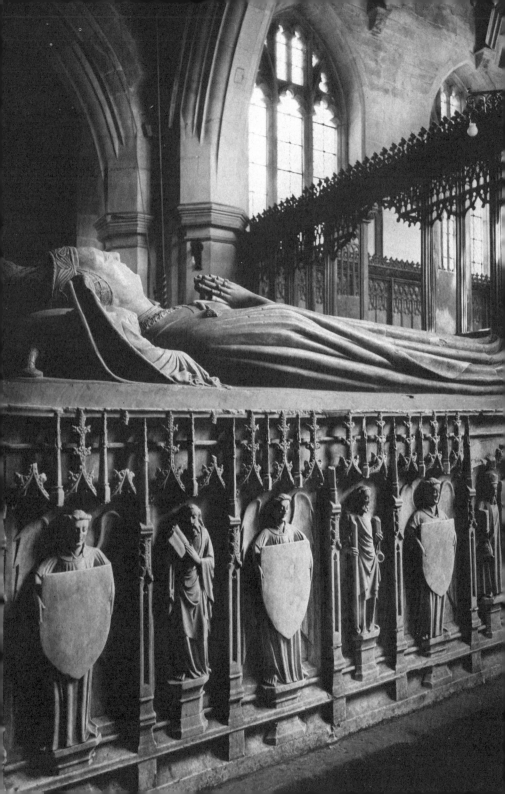

128 (opposite) St Bartholomew, Tong, Shropshire: tomb of Sir Richard and Lady Margaret Vernon

130 (below) St Bartholomew, Quorndon, Leicestershire: detail from the monument of John Farnham

129 (above) St Mary the Virgin, Layer Marney, Essex: tombs of Sir William Marney and Henry, Lord Marney

131 (below) St Peter and St Paul, Kedington, Suffolk: effigy of Grissell Barnardiston

132 (left) All Saints, Stamford, Lincolnshire: brasses of John and Margery Browne

133 (below) St Mary and St Nicholas, Wrangle, Lincolnshire: the Resurrection, detail of the east window

134 (left) St Bartholomew, Quorndon, Leicestershire: tomb-slab of Thomas Farnham and his wife

135 (opposite) St Dunstan, Cranbrook, Kent: south door

CHAPTER FIVE

The Stuart and Georgian periods

THE ELIZABETHAN RELIGIOUS SETTLEMENT achieved a precarious balance of conflicting forces: all were agreed that there could be only one State religion. But in the seventeenth century – a double-faced age, half magical, half scientific, half credulous, half sceptical – this balance in religion could not endure. The last moment of unity was symbolized by the publication in 1611 of the Authorized Version of the Bible, in the translation of which Puritan divines played as large a part as members of the Anglican Church. This harmony between Puritanism, now firmly rooted in English soil, and Anglicanism, which had developed from an ecclesiastical compromise into a true religion dear to many and capable of inspiring a poet of the stature of George Herbert, was inevitably transitory; and the flame of the Old Faith burned the more ardently because its adherents were denied participation in local and national government. It was a situation which bred religious strife and hatred, bloodshed, imprisonment, confiscation. Eventually Civil War broke out between an Anglican King, resting on his predecessors' claims to be Supreme Head of the *Ecclesia Anglicana*, and a Long Parliament of smaller landed gentry and town burgesses and their employees and followers who wanted no priests, no altars, no vestments. Many of them did not even want a national Church.

Under Charles I Archbishop Laud (who might have been called an Anglo-Catholic had the term existed) restored the altar – the most important piece of furniture in the church because of its connection with the Eucharist – to the east end of the chancel and enclosed it with rails to north, west and south. Despite their destruction during the Civil War and Commonwealth, a number of Laudian altar rails survive, for instance at Lyddington, Rutland (where the altar stands a little distance from the east wall and is railed on all four sides) and at Abbey Dore, Herefordshire (where both rails and flamboyant screen were the work of the carpenter John Abel) and at Ranworth, Norfolk. The main object of the rails was *109* to ensure that the altar should be a fixture; its significance in the Laudian church was emphasized by a reredos or tapestry behind it. The parish church of Wigan, Lancashire, still possesses a tapestry dossal of Laudian date made at Mortlake from a cartoon by Raphael depicting the death of Ananias. At St Peter's, Wolverhampton, the Ten Commandments written in gold were placed above the altar, while at Little Gidding in Huntingdonshire the Laudian reredos takes the form of three brass tablets engraved with the Commandments, the Creed and the Lord's Prayer. Wooden boards bearing the same texts were the commonest form of reredos in the following century, as at Petersham, Surrey. *171*

In 1643, however, the House of Commons passed an ordinance abolishing all

136 St Mary the Virgin, Saffron Walden, Essex: Georgian tomb-slabs

altars at the east end and all altar rails. It is remarkable that the church which best
embodies the Laudian ideal was actually built during the Commonwealth:
Staunton Harold, Leicestershire, built by Sir Robert Shirley in his park in 1653.
When Cromwell heard about the new church he ordered Sir Robert to provide
him with a regiment of soldiers on the grounds that if he could afford to build a
church he could afford to pay for a regiment. Sir Robert refused and was
imprisoned in the Tower, where he died.

The spoliation of the religious foundations' properties in the sixteenth century
was the work of envious, worldly-wise men advising a worldly-wise monarch;
but the iconoclasm of Cromwell's fanatical Puritan followers sprang from hatred
of what was thought to be idolatry. It was part of the same attitude that turned
witch-burning from an episode into an epidemic, and that, with the cutting down
of maypoles and the forbidding of sports on the Sabbath, led to the notoriously
gloomy 'English Sunday'. When a weary people turned with relief to the military
dictatorship which restored Charles II, the *Ecclesia Anglicana* appeared much as she
had been organized, and reorganized, by her leading prelates before 1640. But it
was not the same Church, nor were its services and fittings and furniture those of
the earlier single faith.

Chancels were now unimportant; some even fell into ruins. Most of the ritual of
the 'old religion' – priestly vestments, processions, adoration of 'images', and other
elements of the cult in the Middle Ages – had gone. Worse, the people as a nation
were now divided into members of the episcopal Church of England, many of
whom would not conform to the new rules (the original 'non-conformists');
Roman Catholics (heavily penalized); and – newer and stranger – those who had
followed the Scots' Presbyterianism or the German or Swiss Protestantism and
Calvinism in one form or another, the heirs of the Puritans and Commonwealth in
all their jarring sects and beliefs.

For members of the Church of England after 1660 altars were returned to the
158 east end of the chancel and once more railed. But even if the priest still officiated
within the sanctuary, Matins and Evensong were held in naves and communion
was taken at the rails of the sanctuary. In a well-furnished church of the period the
floor of the chancel would be paved with black and white marble and the walls
painted and wainscoted. In London such pavements were almost universal; black
156 and white chancel pavements can also still be seen at Ingestre in Staffordshire,
King's Norton in Leicestershire and Kedington in Suffolk. Fortunately, though
roods had vanished, the chancel screen had been retained under the Royal Order of
1561 and a number of medieval screens survived the Commonwealth. Some new
screens were actually built during the seventeenth and eighteenth centuries. There
137 are examples at Cruwys Morchard in Devonshire, at Croscombe in Somerset and
at Ashburnham in Sussex, while Wren introduced screens at the London churches
of St Margaret Lothbury and St Peter upon Cornhill. The retention of the chancel
screen helped to solve the problem of how to adapt a medieval building for Prayer
Book worship. Instead of dividing the church into 'rooms' used for different
sections of the congregation it now divided them into rooms used for different
services or parts of services.

Apart from the adaptation of medieval churches for the vernacular liturgy and corporate worship, the seventeeth century saw the emergence of a new type of church, usually known as the 'auditory church', designed to accord with the new *p. 180* conception of worship and ritual. The building which first embodied the new plan, and which is also one of the first churches which can be ascribed to a particular architect, was St Paul's Covent Garden (1631), as revolutionary in its *143* classical form as in its arrangement. Its author, Inigo Jones, a Londoner of Welsh descent, had made an intensive and enthusiastic study of Palladio's work in northern Italy and it was he who naturalized the Renaissance style in England. Jones's patron, the Earl of Bedford, asked for nothing much better than a barn – to which the architect replied, 'You shall have the handsomest barn in England.' And in fact the simple Tuscan mass of St Paul's is important not only for the purity of its classical style but also because it *is* like a barn: a single rectangular room with no screen to divide it into chancel and nave, and no arcades. There was originally a railed altar against the east wall. Externally the east wall has a noble blind portico giving on to the grand piazza in the Italian style which was laid out by Jones at the expense of the Earl of Bedford and to the taste of Charles I.

As the sermon had now become the rival of the sacraments, the pulpit was the *137,* most conspicuous piece of furniture. No pains were spared in its adornment and it *159* was surmounted by a majestic sounding-board sometimes as high as the church. The height of the great testered pulpit was, however, partly explained by the height of the square box pews with doors which once furnished nearly all the new *170,* churches: the prominent pulpit enabled the congregation to see and hear the priest *171* over the tops of the tall enclosures. The box pews, of which there is still a splendid array at St Mary at Hill, London, diminished the exaggerated proportions that *164* such pulpits assume in buildings like St Edmund the King and St Clement, Eastcheap in London, where straight low benches have replaced the pews. *159*

The usual form of pulpit in the Georgian period was the three-decker, with the *p. 180* reading desk, and the desk of the clerk who said the responses, attached. The motifs of the carved ornament consisted principally of fruit, flowers and angel heads, as at St Stephen Walbrook and St Mary at Hill, London, motifs which were as *159* evocative of certain aspects of current Christianity as was the old medieval imagery. The same emblems of abundance adorn the fine font covers of the period, all of which are outshone by the exquisite pyramidal group of putti, flowers and fruit at All Hallows, Barking-by-the-Tower, in London. The fonts themselves are *163* smaller than those of the Middle Ages, for the ancient ceremony of immersing the infant was no longer performed. A small bowl on a pedestal sufficed for the revised *181* ceremony. The font might stand in its traditional place, it might furnish a separate room as in the original arrangement at All Saints, Newcastle-upon-Tyne (built in 1789), or in a medieval church a transept might be utilized as a baptistery, as at St Mary Redcliffe in Bristol, for which Thomas Paty made a classical font in 1755.

The practice after the Reformation of setting up the Royal Arms in church became compulsory in 1660. In London's City churches the Royal Arms are *137* among the most striking elements; the vigorous, snarling beasts in St Margaret *162* Pattens are especially impressive. These heraldic creatures are not the only

evidence of worldly concerns in churches of this period: many of them, notably
162 in the City, are adorned with imposing wrought-iron sword-rests for local
dignitaries.

Pews were generally placed so that the congregation faced toward the reading
170 desk and pulpit. This could mean that they were set at all angles (as at Whitby in
Yorkshire), and the striking variety in the design of 'auditory' or pulpit-oriented
churches is to some extent due to the architects' attempts to arrange the interior so
that pulpit, reading desk and altar could be seen by the whole congregation. At All
Saints in Newcastle-upon-Tyne David Stephenson created an elliptical nave to
face an apsidal recess in which pulpit and reading pew were originally placed
180 behind the altar on the chord of the apse. The monumental church of St Chad's at
Shrewsbury, Shropshire, by George Steuart, has a circular nave planned to seat a
large congregation in full sight of both altar and pulpit. Later, at All Souls,
Langham Place in London, John Nash designed a circular vestibule and
colonnaded spire as a picturesque terminal feature to the northward stretch of
Regent Street, but he gave an erratic north-east swing to the nave in order to house
two liturgical centres, enabling the entire congregation to see both the altar and the
grouped pulpit, reading desk and font.

In an age in which the hierarchical structure of society was accepted and in
which Anglicanism had become the upper-class religion it was natural that special
170, prominence should be given to the family pew of the local gentry. The description
177 by Addison of Sir Roger de Coverley in church gives a glimpse of the social aspect
of Anglican worship at that time:

> My friend Sir Roger, being a good Church-man, has beautified the inside of his
> Church with several texts of his own choosing, he has likewise given a
> handsome pulpit cloth and railed in the communion table at his own expense.
> He has often told me that at his coming into his estate he found the Parishioners
> very irregular; and in order to make them kneel and join in the responses, he
> gave every one of them a hassock and a Common-Prayer book; and at the same
> time employed an itinerant singing master, who goes about the country for that
> purpose, to instruct them rightly in the tunes of the Psalms. As Sir Roger is
> landlord to the whole congregation, he keeps them in very good order, and
> suffers no body to sleep in it beside himself; for if by chance he has been surprised
> into a short nap at sermon, upon recovering out of it he stands up and looks
> about him, and if he sees anyone else nodding, either wakes them himself or
> sends his servants to them.

Sometimes a former chantry chapel was used as a family pew, as at Wensley in
Yorkshire and Kedington in Suffolk. Family pews were often fully furnished with
chairs, sofa and a fireplace: the Scrope Pew at Wensley is a sumptuous survival of
177 the so-called parlour pew, and the Bateman Pew at Shobdon, Herefordshire, not
only boasts a fireplace and domestic chairs but has its own entrance from outside.
Parishioners were generally seated in families and paid rent for their pews. Pews
together with the church rates were now the mainstay of parochial finance. But as a
method of seating for an expanding population, the box pew could not continue

indefinitely, and even in its heyday those who could not afford sittings were
relegated with the children to galleries, which often surrounded the interior on
three sides, as at St Martin in the Fields, London, and which also housed the newer
and popular organs at the west end.

162,
164

St Paul's, Covent Garden, foreshadowed the subsequent development of
English church architecture, but it had no immediate followers. It is strange to
think that Staunton Harold, built twenty years later, was the work of masons for
whom the Perpendicular style was still a living tradition and that the Perpendicular
St John's, Briggate, in Leeds (1632) was almost the exact contemporary of Inigo
Jones's Covent Garden church. Gothic architectural forms continued to influence
church-building for some time and the medieval plan was never forgotten. There
is an obvious analogy between a church like St Katharine Cree, in the City's
Leadenhall Street (combining Tuscan columns with a rib vault) or the little church
at Compton Wynyates, Warwickshire (where mullioned windows with trefoil-
headed lights and stepped buttresses consort with a classical entablature) and the
mixed style of that most characteristic prose writer of the age, Sir Thomas
Browne, who used classical images to enforce Christian morals.

The Fire of London in 1666, following upon the Plague of the preceding year,
provided the opportunity to establish the new classical style. An architect equal to
the occasion was at hand. Of the eighty-seven churches lost in the Fire, in addition
to St Paul's Cathedral, it was decided to rebuild fifty. The best vantage-point from
which to gauge Wren's genius is from as high as a doughty enthusiast can climb up
to the golden ball on top of that cathedral. Many of Wren's spires and towers still
stand up as his memorial: *si monumentum requiris, circumspice.*

Wren's 'infinite variety' astonishes. Scarcely any two of his churches look alike,
or were meant to; yet all of them show his power of borrowing classical inspiration
from the Continent and fashioning English materials by English hands to create a
distinctive English Renaissance style; one, moreover, which retained traditional
English features. The sites were irregular, hemmed-in by the old medieval City
lanes and their remaining buildings. But Wren contrived to build all his churches
on two basic themes: the traditional longitudinal church with aisles (as at St Mary
Aldermary) and the simple square or rectangular room to which different
arrangements of columns, domes and vaults give diversity. Except where
Victorian glass has occasionally been inserted, light streams into every corner from
the clear or faintly green panes of ample round- or square-headed windows and of
eye-like ovals and roundels. The whole interior space is visible to all, and each
member of the congregation is fully involved.

161

157,
158

Wren's fertility of imagination shows to perfection in his towers, spires, and
steeples, features looking back to the Early English past, not to the Continent or to
Rome. Frustrated in his scheme to transform the City's street-plan, he succeeded
admirably in transforming its skyline. His towers and spires freely employ both
Gothic and classical motifs with happy effect. At St Vedast, Foster Lane and St
James Garlickhythe, Baroque spires rise from traditional square towers, the former
a dramatic chiaroscuro pattern of flowing convex and concave curves, the latter a

148–
150

149
150

flickering design of urns and columns massed at the corners. These are but two examples in an array of tower compositions which in their tireless invention – making endless play upon geometric motifs, obelisks, stepped truncated pyramids, spheres and cylindrical drums – offer one of the richest of architectural experiences within such a small area.

158   Perhaps Wren's most exalted work, apart from his remarkable cathedral, was his rebuilding of St Stephen's, Walbrook. The plan, unusual for England, consists of a domed central space inscribed in a square: a brilliant display of columns, arches and pendentives then turns the square into a circle above which rises the dome on eight columns. From this central space project a short chancel and transepts to east, north and south, while to west an extra bay gives the edifice some longitudinal sense. In

157   St Magnus the Martyr he is more traditionally classical; but his originality here shows in the dashing circular lights of the clerestory let into the curve of the barrel-roof, and in his genial construction of a majestic altarpiece (restored) in the fashionably shallow chancel.

Wren's most important follower, Nicholas Hawksmoor, introduced an intensely individual sense of drama into church architecture with his bold silhouettes and sculptured masses. He made the most significant contribution to a group of churches built under an Act of Parliament of 1711 providing for 'fifty new churches in and about the City of London and Westminster and Suburbes thereof'. The reason for the Act was not, as might be supposed, the increased population of London, which had trebled during the seventeenth century despite the Plague, but the growing strength of the enemies of the Establishment – Dissent, Popery and active atheism. Churches were necessary to counteract such tendencies.

The actual number built, however, fell far short of the number envisaged by the Act. Of those built, six were designed by Hawksmoor and each is a masterpiece. It is their Roman gravity and grandeur which gives delight, whether it be the heavy voluptuous ornament round the arrestingly tiny doors of St George's-in-the-East and its romantic turrets, or the extraordinary realization of Pliny's description of

151   the tomb of Mausolus in the tower of St George's, Bloomsbury; whether it be the genial play with mammoth stone blocks which make up the strange geometry of

153   St Mary Woolnoth, or the immense breadth and solemnity of the tower of Christ

155   Church, Spitalfields, thrusting up from the Tuscan columns of the ground storey through a bold series of classical stages, niches, arches and lights, to a spire suddenly

59   recalling the Gothic broach spire (it was rebuilt last century without its crockets and lucarnes). Christ Church is, sadly, one of the City's 'redundant' churches, still magnificent in its deplorable ruined state.

Thomas Archer, who was employed to build two of the 'fifty' churches – St

154   John's, Smith Square (1714–28), and St Paul's, Deptford (finished 1720) – was fired by Roman Baroque architecture rather than by ancient Rome. The exterior of St John's, emotional, richly imaginative, dreamlike in the bigness of its scale and detail, is among the noblest sights of London, especially when viewed from the far end of Lord North Street. The vast, romantic, restless church more than spans the width of the reticent Georgian street and looms high above it. The bold square plan is transformed by the aspiring movement of four corner towers, of a vast portico

resting on giant Tuscan columns, and of colossal round-arched windows flanked
by pilasters. St Paul's, Deptford, is equally dramatic, again square in plan, raised on
a great masonry platform like some fortification.

Wren and his immediate followers, though working in the classical style,
created soaring, vertical images which harmonized in spirit with Gothic
architecture. But with the work of James Gibbs, the most potent influence on the
period 1740–60, the essential horizontality of the classical mode is asserted, despite
the Baroque movement of St Mary le Strand (another of the 'fifty' churches).   *168*
Towers were retained by eighteenth-century architects as necessary ingredients of
church-building; indeed their function as belfries had gained in importance after
the Cambridge printer Fabian Stedman introduced change-ringing in 1668. But
they soon ceased to play an integral part in the design. The spire of Gibbs's best-
known church, St Martin in the Fields, when seen from the end of St Martin's Lane   *165*
looks like an afterthought added for the sake of custom, and sits uneasily on the roof
where the west front joins the magnificent Corinthian portico. This steeple was
imitated by Gibbs's pupil Henry Flitcroft at St Giles's-in-the-Fields, by the
unknown architect of the church of Mereworth in Kent, and by church builders in   *166*
North America.

Gibbs treated the classical theme with grace and enthusiasm; so did his followers.
The temple-like churches of the Georgian period – among them Tardebigge in   *167*
Worcestershire (by Francis Hiorn), Over Whitacre and Birley in Warwickshire
(the latter perhaps by Robert Adam), St Lawrence at West Wycombe, Wanstead
in Essex (by Thomas Hardwick), Hardenhuish in Wiltshire (by John Wood the
Younger) and the little apsidal church of All Hallows, London Wall (by George   *174*
Dance the Younger – now the headquarters of the Council for the Care of
Churches) – are infinitely charming. The language they speak is at one in clarity
and commonsense with Locke's philosophy and advocacy of tolerance. It is as
perfectly keyed to its age as was the Early English style to the thirteenth century.

The basically sober and simple forms of Georgian churches were occasionally
invaded by a riot of gilded and stucco ornament, the motifs of which included
secular themes indistinguishable from those found in the multiplying great houses
of the period. The white and gold interior of St Martin in the Fields, with openings
like those of boxes in a theatre looking down into the chancel, is a case in point. But
no English church interior offers a more lavish display of Rococo than Great
Witley in Worcestershire. It was built at the expense of the widow of the first Lord   *172*
Foley, but assumed its present exotic appearance in 1747 when it was altered by the
second Lord Foley. He had purchased the ceiling paintings by Bellucci and the
painted glass at the sale of the contents of Canons, the palatial mansion of the Duke
of Chandos, Handel's patron.

The more characteristic and peculiarly English expression of the Rococo spirit
took the form of Horace Walpole's 'Strawberry Hill Gothic'. At Shobdon in   *175,*
Herefordshire the original Norman church was converted by an unknown   *177*
architect in 1753 for Walpole's friend Lord Bateman into an enchanting toy-
theatre interpretation of a medieval interior. It is as gay as an Austrian Rococo
village church, all white and blue-green with crimson hangings and decorative

ogee arches, which in no way disturb the fundamentally classical lines of the design
and are as remote from true Gothic as the sham ruins in the grounds of
176 contemporary country houses. The interior of Croome d'Abitot, Worcestershire,
is another delightful example of pure Georgian stucco-and-ogee-arched Gothic
and more than hints at the coming revival of the traditional style.

Even when a wholly new theory about the planning and arrangement of
144– churches in the nineteenth century swept away much seventeenth- and eighteenth-
147, century furnishing, the sepulchral monuments of the earlier period remained to
160, evoke its flavour. In their variety these figures in classical settings, accompanied by
172, the characteristic symbolism of flowers, fruits and urns, are among the most
173 absorbing of all the visual treasures of English parish churches. The alabaster
147 likeness of Lady Elizabeth Carey (d. 1620) at Stowe-Nine-Churches in
Northamptonshire, lying in a natural, relaxed attitude with every detail of her
exquisite costume minutely rendered, already shows the realism typical of the
Stuart and Georgian centuries. It was carved by Nicholas Stone, who also made
the uncanny effigy of John Donne, shown standing in his shroud. Puritans looked
askance at effigies, but some fine wall tablets nevertheless date from the time of the
Civil War, among them Edward Marshall's sober bust of the famous William
Harvey at Hempstead, Essex; and in the same decade John Stone carved the
146 extraordinary monument to Sir Edward Spencer at Great Brington, Northamptonshire: he seems to be forcing his way out of his huge funerary urn. The well-
known 'Golden Cavalier', Edward St John, at Lydiard Tregoze in Wiltshire
(1645), stands beneath his canopy as in life, all trace of death or even sleep gone. Sir
Thomas Lucy and his wife at Charlecote, Warwickshire (1640) – he semi-
reclining, she recumbent – shine dazzlingly white among black columns against a
landscape background and a still-life composition of books.

Towards the end of the seventeenth century it became fashionable in portrait
172 sculpture to dress up the subject in Roman costume. An instance of this taste for
Roman attire can be seen at Stamford, Lincolnshire, where John Cecil, fifth Earl of
Exeter, and his wife lie in antique robes on a giant sarcophagus guarded by the
symbolic figures of Grief and Victory. But those who commissioned funeral
effigies nearly always preferred contemporary dress and the eighteenth century
173 abounds in compositions in which bewigged ladies and gentlemen sit, stand or lie
at ease in a framework festooned with putti, fruit and flowers. When the Neo-
classical style became the established mode for monumental sculpture, timeless
draperies took the place of fashionable clothes and the robust portrait gave way to
idealized impersonal features. This trend is already apparent in Banks's famous
182 monument to little Penelope Boothby at Ashbourne, Derbyshire.

In the wonderful array of London parish churches built after the Fire and for a
century and a half thereafter we can see – we cannot avoid seeing – the social and
economic revolution caused by foreign trade, the beginnings of scientific
technology, the better communications (in all media, but especially by sea and
canals) and the first 'urban revolution' which soon came to produce as much of the
national income (i.e. national output) as agriculture itself. This vast social and
economic change, first evident in Holland and England, left country villages with

their big medieval churches but raised in towns and cities lively new, yet classical, monuments to an Age of Reason, and of reasoned and reasonable religion.

Indeed, English life underwent a vast, second, silent revolution in the ninety years between the Restoration in 1660 and the middle of the eighteenth century. The better-known political revolutions of the Civil War and the civil overthrow of James II in 1688–89 masked the slow but steady scientific and technological revolution in English thought, religion and everyday work which unfolded between the Commonwealth and the first stirrings of the much better-known so-called Industrial Revolution after 1750. Up to the first half of the eighteenth century England's agriculture, though slowly improved in the sixteenth and seventeenth centuries, remained much as it always had been in methods; so English villages and their people's lives and livelihood, like their buildings and dresses, also improved and changed only gradually.

With the birth of the Royal Society under the Commonwealth (its charter came with the Restoration), reorganization of Charles II's Navy (largely by Samuel Pepys), foundation of the Bank of England under William and Mary, and widespread application of the results of the first really scientific inquiries in agriculture, communications, navigation, building and other techniques and crafts, English life began its big turn-around, from an economy that was essentially agrarian and rural to one that was industrial and urban. The fairly rapid change (in historical terms) caused vast social changes as the old squirearchy and traditional village life – a legacy from Anglo-Saxon times – ran down in magnitude and amplitude, and the commercial-industrial urban life (with employer-employee relationships divorced from the older craft guild hierarchical relationships) expanded, to explode into full-blown urban industrialism and commerce with the real Industrial Revolution after Waterloo.

English literature records this in Restoration comedy, in *The Spectator*, in Oliver Goldsmith's prose and poetry ('The Deserted Village' tells its own tale, not only of Ireland but even more of England), and throughout the great eighteenth-century novelists' works; yet one can trace the silent economic and social revolution much earlier, in John Bunyan and Defoe, long before Swift, Fielding, Sterne, Richardson and finally Jane Austen. The eighteenth century saw not only the eclipse of Sir Roger de Coverley and his fellow squires; it also saw the run-down of many village churches, grass growing in their aisles, their pews worm-eaten. A comparatively low standard of ecclesiastical duties and widespread pluralism are reflected in the wonderfully vivid diaries of the Rev. James Woodforde. But the picture is by no means entirely gloomy. Parson Woodforde worked his own glebe, and this and the receipt of his tithes kept him in close touch with agricultural life:

1776. Sept. 14. Very busy all day with my barley, did not dine till 5 in the after noon, my harvest men dined here today, gave them some beef and some plumb pudding and as much liquer as they would drink. . . . Dec. 3rd. My Frolic for my people to pay tithe to me this day. I gave them a good dinner, surloin of beef roasted, a leg of mutton boiled and plumb puddings in plenty.

The improvement of agriculture and the rise in the value of tithes had helped the clergy, who had been impoverished in the seventeenth century owing to high prices and the difficulty of obtaining their full tithe in kind, especially in towns. Throughout the eighteenth century country gentlemen came more and more to regard livings in their gift as worth the acceptance of their younger sons. Jane Austen makes it clear that by her time the ideal arrangement was a handsome rectory built in a pleasant spot not too far from the manor house and inhabited by a son of the squire.

But for the first time since Christianity claimed the English a millennium and more earlier, the life and works of the Church of England entered a long phase of perfunctory worship. Village church-going became mainly a matter of social status, conformity, fashion and propriety. One must emphasize the word 'village' here because, with the new urban commercial classes and their employees, in newly designed or re-designed churches (in which chancels tended to be omitted, since there was less ritual to fill them), the Church of England had much success; though that very success later led to charges that the Church and its ministers were too worldly, had forgotten the common people, and had also turned their backs on the age-long mysteries and ritual of the Christian Church as a whole. Part of these charges was true, especially in English villages, save only where some ideal squire or other estate-owner poured both his substance and his faith into proper premises, parsons, and other provisions for his villagers' and neighbours' spiritual sustenance. The State was now doing more in villages, through the law, which put upon local magistrates much of the duties of looking after the poor, removing vagabond (unemployed) workpeople who did not belong to the parish, and even regulating prices and wages. Out of all this – as the rational, reasonable, commercial, urbanizing eighteenth century unfolded – came the new Dissenters and Nonconformists associated with the Wesleys, Whitefield, and many another who led their flocks out of the Church into new pastures and new pastoral directions.

In this silent social and economic revolution, between 1660 and 1750, village life began to empty its young, bolder and more ambitious souls into the fast-growing towns and, later, seaboard and industrial cities; so began the trek towards modern urban English life. It was only natural that along with this revolution, with the accusations against an easy-going Church, should arise not only new doctrines but also a new style. With the swing-back to ritual and ancient Christian fundamentals came a new style of church architecture called, appropriately, 'Gothic Revival'. There is far, far more in that term than meets an eye looking merely at style.

Notes on the plates

136 St Mary the Virgin, Saffron Walden, Essex: Georgian tomb-slabs
Almost all church floors which have escaped Victorian tiling are partly paved with tomb-slabs (see also Didmarton, pl. 48). Before the seventeenth century burial within the church was limited; but by 1682 the diarist John Evelyn could deplore as unhygienic 'the custom of burying every-one within the body of the church'. The wealthier the deceased, the nearer he might approach to the most coveted place of sepulchre, the chancel. The position of the slabs shown here, at the west end of the nave, reflects the comparatively humble status of the deceased.

The light-reflecting material of which the slabs are made is Belgian slate, or 'touch', which was introduced into this country after the Reformation.

137 St Mary, Croscombe, Somerset: interior, looking east
The medieval church was refurnished in the early seventeenth century and shows the method of arranging a post-Reformation interior. The Royal Order of 1561 had insisted on the retention of screens, with the exception of the parts above the rood loft. The medieval screen at Croscombe had been destroyed, and the present proud, exotic structure with its two tiers of arches, its strapwork and obelisks, replaced it in 1616. The lavishly framed Royal Arms take the place of the medieval rood. The prominent pulpit stands against the pier one bay west of the screen, as was usual after the Reformation and before the Restoration. The tester or sounding-board above it, intended to magnify the speaker's voice, became an important item of decoration in the seventeenth and eighteenth centuries (see, for instance, pls. 156, 159, 170).

138, 139 St Mary, Leighton Bromswold, Huntingdonshire: west front and view across the transept
When the poet George Herbert first held the prebend of Leighton, the medieval church lay in ruins. According to John Ferrar's *Life* of his famous brother, Herbert's friend Nicholas Ferrar of Little Gidding, 'the Vicar and Parish were fain to use my Lord Duke's great Hall for yr Prayers & preaching'. Herbert then 'set upon it to sollicite his Friends, spared not his own Purse So God in the end blessed both yr Endeavours, that a handsome and uniforme (& as the Country termed it) a fine neat Church was erected, Inside and outside finished not only to yr Parishioners own much comfort and joy, but to the admiration of all men.' The work was begun in 1632 to George Herbert's specifications and under the supervision of John Ferrar.

Despite the pinnacles in the form of classical ball-topped obelisks and the classical window openings, the exterior looks Gothic. The interior, though now bereft of the plaster and texts which once covered the walls, and lit by oil lamps instead of candles, retains all its robust Carolean woodwork, which by comparison with the fanciful work at Croscombe (pl. 137) is as sober and purposeful as Herbert's reflections on the parts of the church and the church service in *The Temple*. Its extraordinary interest derives not only from its associations but from its unaltered aspect as a church 're-edified and refurnished' for early seventeenth-century Anglican worship. In his *Life* of Herbert, Izaac Walton says: 'By his order the reading pew and pulpit' (both seen on the right in pl. 139, one on each side of the chancel arch) 'were a little distant from each other, and both of an equal height; for, he would often say, They should neither have a precedency or priority

171

of the other; but that prayer and preaching, being equally useful, might agree like brethren, and have an equal honour and estimation.'

Herbert divided the nave and chancel by a partition about five feet high which is a compromise between the traditional screen and the rails which Laudian churchmen liked to set across the chancel.

140 St Mary, Bromfield, Shropshire: chancel ceiling
Apart from delineating the Royal Arms and adorning the walls with texts (pl. 112), the painter had little scope in an Anglican church until after the Restoration. Then the ceiling over the chancel was often decorated to give emphasis to the altar and the place where the communicants assembled. Thus Bromfield not only has a magnificent Royal Arms painted on the south wall of the nave, but this most engaging pattern of cloud, fluttering angels and text-bearing streamers in brown, red and silvery grey in the chancel. It was done by a local artist, Thomas Francis, in 1672. In the centre is the traditional diagram of the Trinity: at the points of the triangle are the Father, Son and Holy Ghost; each is God (at the centre) and God is all three, but they are not the same as each other.

141 St John the Baptist, Halifax, West Riding of Yorkshire: window in the south choir aisle
The clear Commonwealth glass replaced a medieval window. The hated idolatrous images have gone, but the window is still full of life, most especially when winter sun flames the uneven crown glass. To that sparkle is added the movement of the shifting shapes of the leading – star forms spreading beyond the circles attempting to confine them, to merge into multiple diamond patterns, and restrained at last only by the decorative borders of lozenges and rectangles.

142 St Mary, Oxford: south porch
143 St Paul, Covent Garden, London: portico
The two porches, both dating from the 1630s, dramatically announce the divergent aspects of the classical mode which were to affect church-building for nearly 200 years. The Oxford porch (1637), so curiously

attached to a Perpendicular church, and even more curiously disclosing a fan-vaulted interior, speaks the turbulent language of Baroque adopted by Hawksmoor and John James – though the Roman ideas are here coloured by Flemish love of ornament. The London portico (1631–38) by Inigo Jones heralds the composed and stately Palladianism of the later Georgian Period.

The Oxford porch is attributed to Nicholas Stone, who appears again in these pages as a funeral sculptor (pl. 147). With its twisted columns, its niche thrusting through a broken pediment and huge volutes low down at the sides, it is like the architectural frontispieces of books of the period; and perhaps Stone may have seen Raphael's cartoon of *The Healing of the Lame Man*, bought by Charles I about 1630, which shows two huge twisting columns based on a column in St Peter's at Rome which was thought to come from Solomon's Temple.

Inigo Jones's portico is not, surprisingly, the entrance to his church: it adorns the east end, and was designed to form part of his arcaded piazza of Covent Garden.

144 St Mary, Harefield, Middlesex: monuments of Alice Spencer, Countess of Derby, and Sophia, Lady Newdigate
Harefield is one of those churches – Kedington in Suffolk is another (pl. 130) – where the array of sepulchral art is so breathtaking that it is difficult to attend to other details, even though the furnishings here, the box pews, the elaborate pulpit and the extraordinary Decalogue reredos of frosted glass, are of exceptional interest. The Countess, who died in 1636, lies in a gaudy, canopied four-poster guarded by predatory heraldic griffons and surmounted by her coat of arms. Thick, crumpled curtains are looped back to reveal the bold, crowned, brightly painted effigy.

The juxtaposition of this insistent image, as brassy as a fairground organ figure, and the white classical urn of Lady Newdigate (d. 1774), standing in a simple black niche, is one of the more arresting of those contrasts in which parish churches abound. The urn, one of three, is crowned by the figure of Death in the gentle guise of a winged boy and carved with the delicate shallow relief of a reclining nymph holding a garland symbolizing the resurrection.

145 St Peter and St Paul, Borden, Kent: wall monument of Robert Plot
The unusual allegorical imagery – the background of spears, cannon and cannon-balls and the charming Italianate figure of St Michael gracefully subduing the Devil – and the excellence of the carving make this monument the most arresting object in the church. Attributed to Jasper Latham, it commemorates Robert Plot (d. 1671), father of Dr Plot, the historian of Stafford-shire and Oxfordshire (see note 156).

146 Great Brington, Northamptonshire: monument of Sir Edward Spencer
This life-size half-figure rising from an urn – an urn-burial resurrection – is strange enough to startle the most seasoned church-crawler. Sir Edward, who died in 1656 (1655 Old Style), rests his left hand on the Bible on the column of Truth, while to his right stands the square pillar of the Word of God. This is one of the comparatively few monuments set up during the Com-monwealth. The sculptor was John Stone, son of Nicholas (see pls. 142, 147).

147 St Michael, Stowe-Nine-Churches, Northamptonshire: monument of Elizabeth, Lady Carey
The effigy was carved in lady Carey's lifetime, about 1620, by Nicholas Stone, and is an early instance of an authenticated funerary portrait. Realism in the portrayal of likenesses became more and more marked in the seventeenth and eighteenth centuries. If the portrait effigy was not modelled or carved from life it was usually taken from a painting after the subject's death. Not only is the whole relaxed pose of the figure completely natural, but the realism extends to the minute and exquisite detail of the subject's dress and of the embroidered and tasselled cushion resting on griffons beneath her head.

148 St Mary le Bow, London: steeple
149 St Vedast, Foster Lane, London: steeple
150 St James Garlickhythe, London: steeple
These three designs alone would be enough to prove the irrepressible fertility of Wren's invention and his remarkable genius for synthesis. However various in their upper stages, they all rise over a square plan like their medieval predecessors: the difference in style between the former Gothic and the seventeenth-century classical modes is skilfully bridged by constant reference to the past. The glorious tower of St Mary le Bow (1670–80) is basically a traditional steeple encased in classical trimmings – colonnades, balustrades and conspicuous volutes used with brilliant originality to recall the medieval flying buttress. In the spectacular steeple of St Vedast (1694–97), the curving sides alternate between convex and concave until they reach the spire, flowing together in an exciting chiaroscuro pattern which gives the same sense of dynamic upward growth as the spire of Ketton (pl. 59). As for the spire of St James Garlickhythe (1713–17), it looks and is remote from any Gothic design, yet its three stages, made one by flickering urns, columns massed at the corners and huge angle volutes, form a silhouette vibrating with a movement and an emotion which relate it in feeling to a spire such as Newark (pl. 58).

The names of City churches are as distinctive as their architecture. St James, not unexpectedly, stands near a place where garlic was sold. St Mary le Bow takes its name from the arched crypt over which its eleventh-century predecessor was built. St Vedast or Vedastus was a sixth-century bishop saint of Arras in northern France, whose name was pronounced Va-astus, hence the variant name of the church, St Foster.

151 St George, Bloomsbury, London: steeple
The stages of Hawksmoor's astonishingly individual tower and steeple (1723), unlike those of Wren, are completely distinct, and instead of referring to native Gothic tradition the forms allude to historical Antiquity. The stepped pyramid of the steeple, set on a stage composed of four pedimented porticos, is based on a drawing of the Mausoleum at Halicarnassus, but the classical tomb has been converted into a giant pedestal for a Roman altar surmoun-ted by a statue of George I. Originally a life-size lion and unicorn fought for the crown below the statue, but they were taken down in the nineteenth century as 'very doubtful ornaments'.

152 St Michael Cornhill, London: view from the south
Wren built the body of the church (refaced by Sir Gilbert Scott in 1857–60), and the lower part of the tower had survived the Great Fire. Hawksmoor designed the upper part of the tower (1718–19), and here he follows Wren's example in his reference to medieval precedent. However, where Wren invests classical forms with the Gothic spirit, Hawksmoor gives a visual impression of Gothic forms by combining round-arched windows and sharply divided stages with huge fantastic pepperpot pinnacles incongruously topped by flaming urns.

153 St Mary Woolnoth, London: west front
This church, built in 1716–24, shows Hawksmoor in a very different mood. Wren several times declared his sense of the importance of geometry: 'Beauty is from Geometry', he wrote, and 'Firmness, Commodity and Delight, Beauty and Strength depend upon the geometrical Reasons of Opticks and Staticks.' But it was Hawksmoor, not Wren, who created, in St Mary Woolnoth, the most formidable of all exercises in geometry. Severely square and rectangular forms, huge rustication and giant keystones create a deceptive re-semblance to a simple construction of toy bricks. But the treatment of the façade is an amazing play upon the theme of twin western towers. The theme is merely suggested by the gaping rectangular opening dividing the second stage of the projection into two pilastered oblongs, then clearly emerges in the square separate oblongs set above their common entablature.

154 St John, Smith Square, London, seen from Lord North Street
155 Christ Church, Spitalfields, London: west front
In these two wonderful churches, St John by Thomas Archer (1714–28) and Christ Church by Nicholas Hawksmoor (1714–29), the outstanding characteristic of Baroque architecture, bigness of scale, is spectacularly present. St John not only towers above its surroundings: the portico towards which we are looking is wider than the street. As for Christ Church, it reduces

even the five-storey warehouse on the right to pigmy size.
The restless upward movement of the façade at the end of Lord North Street begins with the portico steps and the gigantic pillars and continues beyond the cornice in an open-pedimented structure that breaks through a balustrade and rises to thrust through the great broken pediment of the whole front. The huge corner towers carry the design yet higher.
The strikingly novel feature of Hawksmoor's colossal church is the portico, which consists of an arch between two rectangular openings and is thus shaped like a vast Palladian window. Variations on the same theme occur on the next two stages of the tower, which terminates in a broach spire (compare pl. 59) that was originally more ornate, with classicizing lucarnes, rows of crockets along the ridges, and a large finial at the top.
St John and Christ Church are among the less than twenty churches actually built under the Act of 1711 that called for fifty new churches. Another is St Mary le Strand (pl. 168), whose architect, James Gibbs, served with Hawksmoor as Surveyor for the Commissioners.

156 St Mary, Ingestre, Staffordshire: interior, looking east
157 St Magnus the Martyr, London: interior: looking south-east
The robust plaster reliefs of beribboned swags, flowers and fruit that encrust the ceilings of nave and chancel at Ingestre and the rich carving on the screen and pulpit have their counterparts in sumptuous domestic interiors such as Easton Neston, Belton and Chatsworth. But Wren (almost certainly the architect) uses these secular, classical details in the service of a medieval church pattern of aisled nave and projecting chancel. This and the clustered shafts of the piers show the same awareness of tradition as the City church towers. As at Croscombe sixty years earlier (pl. 137), the Royal Arms occupy the position of the rood above the chancel screen.
St Magnus is planned as an auditory church with no projecting chancel, and its atmosphere is altogether different from that of the Staffordshire building. There, despite the medieval plan, the design is markedly

horizontal, the forms static: at St Magnus, the architecture is animated by that sense of aspiration which links Gothic and Baroque. The height and slenderness of the columns, the lofty curve of the barrel vault, the arches into which the circular clerestory windows are let and the deep, light-filled penetrations from them, like reflections in water, set the whole interior in vertical motion. The circular openings at Ingestre, recalling and perhaps inspired by those of Alberti's San Francesco at Rimini, merely decorate and stress the horizontality of the frieze-like clerestory.

The two churches were built at almost the same time, St Magnus in 1671–85, Ingestre in 1676. The consecration of the latter in 1677 and the splendid dinner given by the lord of the manor, Walter Chetwynd, to follow it are described in detail by Dr Robert Plot, Secretary of the Royal Society and author of a history of Staffordshire.

158 St Stephen Walbrook, London: view from the chancel to the north transept
With immense ingenuity Wren here converted a simple rectangle into a domed cruciform church, built in 1672–77. The dome is borne by eight arches of which we can see parts of four, and these arches rest on twelve identical columns grouped in threes. Arches, vaults and dome are made of wood and plaster; the whole spatial masterpiece depends, like the effects of Continental Baroque interiors, on illusion and on the mystery of constantly changing vistas. Against the wall of the chancel, at the extreme right, Wren's grand reredos of dark oak survives.

159 St Clement, Eastcheap, London: font and pulpit
The handsome font was placed near the pulpit rather than at the west end of the church to accord with a Puritan preference, and so that baptism might be truly congregational (as at Petersham, pl. 171). The rich, voluted font-cover and the towering pulpit with its crown of little cherubs were carved by Jonathan Mayne, who also worked in both wood and stone at St Paul's Cathedral. The small and simple church was built by Wren in 1683–87.

160 Holy Cross and St Mary, Quainton, Buckinghamshire: monument of Richard and Anne Winwood
This is the earliest signed work (1691) by one of the most important sculptors of the period, Thomas Stayner, a Londoner, who like so many of the remarkable authors of parish church monuments was trained in a local mason's yard. The husband and wife are presented with vivid realism, Richard reclining while Anne half rises by his side to watch over him.

161 St Mary Aldermary, London: nave and aisle vaults
A parishioner, Henry Rogers, donated £5,000 for the rebuilding of this church after the Fire on condition that the new St Mary should repeat the Perpendicular style of the old. At a superficial glance Wren's interior, finished in 1682 – the piers, the four-centred clerestory lights, the fan vaults – do indeed look like authentic early sixteenth-century work. But in fact this is a free version rather than a copy of an older church. The vault is more like that of the eighteenth-century Saloon at Arbury Hall, Warwickshire, than that of the Lane Aisle at Cullompton (pl. 114), for it is of plaster, and between the fans are charming little saucer domes completely alien to the Gothic spirit.

162 St Margaret Pattens, London: Stuart Arms and organ
The pipes of the mid eighteenth-century organ are grouped like shafted columns above the prominent and superbly carved Royal Arms, installed when the church was built (1684–87) and James II was on the throne. Although Royal Arms made their appearance in all parish churches after the Reformation to represent the union of Church and State, they seldom played a major part in sixteenth-century church decoration. In the City churches, however, the Royal Arms are often among the most striking objects in the interior, insisting upon the duties of earthly citizenship. The splendidly vigorous lion and unicorn here snarl and toss their golden manes, ready at any moment to leap across the heraldic interval that divides them.

St Margaret has been associated since the fifteenth century with the Worshipful Company of Pattenmakers, producers of galoshes and platform-soled overshoes that kept their wearers up out of the filth of unpaved streets.

163 All Hallows, Barking-by-the-Tower, London: font-cover
This staggering wood carving, for which a contract of 1682 with Grinling Gibbons has recently been found, exalts the imagery which gradually took the place of the forbidden figures of saints and angels after the Reformation. Cherubs, roses, dog daisies, forget-me-nots and tulips, splitting peapods, oak and chestnut leaves, crowned by an alighting dove, these emblems of fruitfulness, fulfilment and peace extol the joys of this world and the next, expressing a duality which is deeply characteristic of the City churches.
The font that it was made to cover served for the christening of William Penn in 1644, and in 1697 was presented to the newly founded Christ Church at Philadelphia.

164 St Mary at Hill, London: interior, looking south-west
The photograph shows another finely carved Royal Arms, some of the only box pews to survive in a Wren City church, their relation to one of the high-based columns and, most conspicuously, the elaborate wrought-iron sword-rests intended for the sword of the Lord Mayor when he visited the church in state. St Mary at Hill possesses no less than six of these emphatically worldly objects, one of them the gift of Alderman Beckford, father of the author of *Vathek* and builder of Fonthill. The delicate ironwork climbs and coils about heraldic and military devices, rising in each of the two examples we can see here to support the Royal Crown in whose name and for whose defence swords were worn. In addition, the sword-rest on the right is supported by dragons, the City's symbolic beasts. The earliest sword-rests were of wood like those in St Helen, Bishopsgate and St Mary Aldermary: the first dated wrought-iron example is at St Magnus and is of 1708.

165 St Martin in the Fields, London: view from the south-west
In the short time which elapsed between the erection of St Mary le Strand (pl. 168) and

the designing of St Martin in the Fields, finished in 1726, Gibbs's mood and that of his age changed to one of cool rationalism and commonsense. St Martin, built on a site where the architect had actually found Roman remains, is a classical temple with a splendidly pagan Corinthian portico, complete without its steeple, which sits grotesquely on the low-pitched roof. The church's widespread influence − which reached as far as the colonies in North America − shows how perfectly it was attuned to the climate of English eighteenth-century Protestantism. It was not one of the churches covered by the Act of 1711, but was financed by the parishioners.

166 St Lawrence, Mereworth, Kent: view from the south-west
Built for John Fane, Earl of Westmorland, in about 1740 by an unknown architect, St Lawrence is an often quoted example of St Martin's influence. But it is interesting to see how the steeple, by repeating the forms of its prototype in sombre-coloured stone and with different, elongated proportions, seems to be forcing its way through the roof rather than resting upon it and thus gives the impression of consistent verticality. The body of the church and the semicircular portico have the wide, deliberately primitive eaves and unfluted columns which, according to the ancient Roman writer Vitruvius, characterized the Tuscan or Etruscan temple. The style was introduced into England by Inigo Jones's St Paul, Covent Garden (pl. 143).

167 St Bartholomew, Tardebigge, Worcestershire: view from the south-east
The Baroque element emerges again in Francis Hiorn's tower of 1777 which, although it is not possible to see the whole of it in the photograph, is a true tower rising from the ground. The ball-topped needle spire is medieval in outline and consorts intriguingly with the concave walls, urns and jutting angle pilasters of the bell stage.

168 St Mary le Strand, London
St Mary le Strand, begun in 1714, was one of the first churches to be built under the Act of 1711 for fifty new churches (see p. 166). The architect was James Gibbs, with

Hawksmoor Surveyor to the Commissioners for these new churches – until he was dismissed in 1716 as a Papist and a Jacobite. When he designed St Mary's he had recently returned from Rome, and this may partly account for the strongly vertical, Baroque spirit of the building. Basically rectangular, banded about with unusually prominent cornices and with a semicircular west porch, the church yet seems in its extreme narrowness to shoot upwards with a dynamic flurry of niche, urn, flaming torch, pediment and parapet to the four stages of its high pilastered tower and lantern. Like a tall-masted ship, towing St Clement Danes behind it, it cleaves the stream of traffic.

169 St Mary, Leebotwood, Shropshire: interior, looking east
A medieval interior transformed by the clear glass and comfortable box pews of the Georgian era. The pews are furnished with iron pegs for the parishioners' coats. A low partition replaces the former screen. The reading pew still stands next to the pulpit where the minister could best be heard. On most Sunday mornings in the eighteenth century the whole service was taken from the reading desk. The only false note in this cosy, reassuring room is struck by the harsh Victorian floor tiles.

170 St Mary, Whitby, North Riding of Yorkshire: interior, looking south-east
This interior comes as a delightful surprise after the massive and rather forbidding external aspect of a medieval church, with some Georgian windows, standing bleakly high above the town and the sea. At first we seem to be looking at an exciting jumble of galleries and pews (dating from the early seventeenth to the eighteenth century), sliding this way and that and reaching almost to the ceiling. Then, gradually, the arrangement is seen to have a certain logic. The box pews, which in many cases lead one into another with a maze-like effect, are so arranged that their occupants can all see the high pulpit with its unusual sounding-board crowned with scrolly leaf fronds and a pineapple. Pulpit and reading desk are combined in this three-tiered structure, dated 1778, of which the bottom storey is the so-called 'vicarage pew', intended for the parson's family

There is no true screen in this church: in 1720 the authorities in the diocese of York, for no known reason, ordered the removal of a great many screens, and that at Whitby was among them. The distinction between the bright nave and the dark, Norman chancel is, however, maintained by a 'flying pew', the Cholmondeley Pew, rising on barley-sugar columns. The gulf dividing the Georgian from the medieval church could scarcely be more forcibly illustrated than by this substitution of a family pew for the rood and rood loft.

171 All Saints, Petersham, Surrey: interior, looking east
The east end of this charming church, which still bears traces of its thirteenth-century origin, shows as typical a Georgian arrangement as the Whitby nave. A fine wrought-iron balustrade accompanies the steps leading to the upper stage of a two-decker pulpit, and the pulpit commands a dignified array of panelled box pews all painted white inside like those seen in the foreground of the photograph. This is a church with a single liturgical centre, so the font stands at the east end, where the congregation could watch the christening ceremony after the second lesson at Matins or Evensong. Behind the altar are the usual boards lettered with the Commandments, the Creed and the Lord's Prayer. There was formerly also a picture in front of the window, painted on such fine canvas that it was transparent. It was, most interestingly, an expression of the taste of the time rather than biblical, for it showed a Gothic ruin in a landscape.

172 St Michael, Great Witley, Worcestershire: monument of the first Lord Foley in the transept
As we have seen, the conventionalized tomb-figures of the early Middle Ages soon gave way to images that appear fully in the round in all their earthly finery (pl. 128), then rise from a recumbent position to kneel (pl. 130) or stand erect, or assume easy life-like attitudes – sometimes, as at Quorndon (pl. 129), with episodes from their lives carved in relief beside them. Rysbrack's spectacular monument to the first Lord Foley, who died in 1743, illustrates a further development: the effigy itself becomes part of a theatrical three-dimensional com-

position, posed against a pyramid symbolic of immortality. The taste of the time is reflected in the classical dress worn by all the animated figures except the widow. It was a fashion which Rysbrack, a prolific and influential sculptor, did much to encourage. His career is an early instance of the specialization which was beginning to separate the professions of architect and sculptor.

In the church, built before 1735 by an unknown architect and decorated after 1747, we see fancy-dress Rococo instead of the 'Gothick' of its contemporary Shobdon (pl. 175), which results in a deepening of the near-secular atmosphere common to both. The ornament covering the whole church was carried out in *papier maché* from moulds of the Italian stucco work at Canons, the Duke of Chandos's mansion near London, from which the glass and ceiling paintings at Great Witley also came.

173 Holy Cross and St Mary, Quainton, Buckinghamshire: monument of Mr Justice Dormer
As at Great Witley (pl. 172), but some fifteen years earlier – Mr Justice Dormer died in 1728 – instead of a tomb we see a theatrical composition, here set against a stage-like architectural background, a great pedimented arch filled with a symbolic pyramid and cloud-borne angels. The subject of this tableau is the agony of grief. There is no attempt to represent the deceased as he was in life, whether asleep or active: he is shown with gripping realism, gaunt, half covered by a blanket, immediately after death, while his mother weeps over him and his periwigged father makes a gesture of despair. The drama of the scene is heightened by the contrast between the white figures and the variegated marble of the background and sarcophagus. The author of this magnificent and moving group is not known.

174 All Hallows, London Wall, London: chancel
By comparison with the interiors of Great Witley (pl. 172) and Shobdon (pl. 175), this tiny church – designed by George Dance the Younger in 1765, when he was only twenty-four – seems particularly chaste. But the longer one looks at the design, the

more its Neo-classical simplicity is seen to be the result of exquisite sophistication. The sparse ornament, flat and delicate by comparison with earlier work, is excitingly varied in scale; the windows are placed high up, and the barrel vault into which they are set rests, surprisingly, not on a cornice but directly on a frieze, which unites Ionic pilasters, windows and apse.

175 St John the Evangelist, Shobdon, Herefordshire: interior, looking west
A previous note touches on the mood of clarity, of steady serenity embodied in St Martin in the Fields (pl. 165) as opposed to the emotional, aspiring, richly imaginative quality of a church such as St John, Smith Square (pl. 154). At Shobdon and in the churches we shall be looking at next (pls. 176–179) the clarity and sanity combine with such lightness and gaiety of form that it is difficult not only to associate them with the mysteries of religion but to regard them as likely settings for Anglican worship. The original Norman Shobdon was Gothicized in 1752–56 for the lord of the manor, the Hon. Richard Bateman, a friend of Horace Walpole. And the relationship between Strawberry Hill and the quatrefoils, cusps, quivering crockets and ogee arches of this scintillating stucco interior is manifest. Once the eye is accustomed to the Gothick delights of Shobdon it becomes apparent, looking through the great ogee curves of the chancel arch, that, like Petersham, this church has a single liturgical centre. The three-storeyed, ornate pulpit, the Norman font and the lectern are grouped about the central space of the crossing, leaving a clear view of the altar. Visible at the far left is the Bateman family pew (pl. 178).

176, 179 St Mary Magdalene, Croome d'Abitot, Worcestershire: interior, looking west, and view from the south-west
The interior of Croome d'Abitot, built in 1763, is perhaps by Robert Adam, who worked on Croome Court. Like Shobdon, it is a basically horizontal design Gothick trimmed. The tall, clustered columns support an entablature which is wholly classical. The delicate plaster decoration on the coved ceiling of the nave and the flat ceilings of the aisles fancifully suggests rather than counterfeits Gothic motifs.

The exterior of Croome d'Abitot gives evidence of a rather more serious appreciation of true Gothic. The battlemented nave with Decorated windows, the pinnacles, pierced parapet, buttresses and traceried bell window of the tower (filled with a version of Somerset tracery: compare pl. 99) are almost convincing. But the tall arches in the ground stage, the proportions of the storeys and the strong emphasis on the string-courses are eighteenth-century rather than medieval. And even in the photograph the site of the church, in open grassland with not a tombstone in sight, seems odd. The building was probably designed by Capability Brown and was conceived as a Picturesque incident in the park he laid out for Lord Coventry of Croome Court, so it is set on a rise where it can be seen from the house.

177 St John the Evangelist, Shobdon, Herefordshire: Bateman Pew
This family pew occupies the south transept of the church (see pl. 175), while opposite it in the north transept was the servants' pew. The photograph concentrates on the Gothick chairs and the fantastic fireplace, where Gothic and classic motifs mingle as vivaciously as they do in the hybrid Jacobean fireplaces at Bolsover Castle, though there the classical idiom was in the ascendant, while here the Gothic is beginning to oust the classic.

178 St Mary, Tetbury, Gloucestershire: interior, looking north-west
Built in 1781 by Francis Hiorn, who has figured in these pages as the architect of Tardebigge (pl. 167), St Mary's is of the same decade as Wyatt's legendary Fonthill, and it discloses the same Picturesque preoccupation with scale in its exaggerated height, the exaggerated slenderness of its piers (made possible by cast-iron cores), the exaggerated tallness of the pier bases, and the strange effects of proportion achieved by the placing of the gallery. At Fonthill Wyatt wanted his Gothic authentic and solid. Hiorn's huge traceried windows suggest that this was his intention too: yet St Mary's is no more archaeologically correct than Fonthill: the core remains classical and the rib vault is of course of plaster.

179 St Mary Magdalene, Croome d'Abitot, Worcestershire: view from the south-west.
See pl. 176

180 St Chad, Shrewsbury, Shropshire: nave
George Steuart's circular design for his Shrewsbury nave (1792) boldly attempts to provide a clear view of the officiating minister for every member of a large congregation. The photograph shows the grand sweep of the nave cornice echoing the gallery balustrade, and the delightful contrast between the smooth, simple Ionic columns carrying the gallery and the extremely tall, attenuated fluted Corinthian columns that support the ceiling. As at Tetbury (pl. 178), their form was made possible by the use of cast iron, a novelty due here to Steuart's collaboration with an engineer, John Simpson, the builder of the Caledonian Canal. Such partnerships were eventually to change the whole character of the profession of architecture.

181 St Swithun, Worcester: font
The fonts of St Clement, Eastcheap and All Saints, Petersham (pls. 159, 171) were prominent objects at the focal centre of the church. The position of the font of 1736 at St Swithun reflects the opposite belief – that different parts of the church should be used for different services. It is set in the middle of a square pew known as the christening pew, with seats for the christening party along the sides. The font's diminutive size proclaims the post-Reformation rejection of baptism by total immersion.

182 St Oswald, Ashbourne, Derbyshire: monument of Penelope Boothby in the Boothby Chapel
Little Penelope Boothby, who died in 1791, lies in a naturalistic attitude of sleep, wears contemporary dress and is an actual portrait; but the figure lacks the sharp definition and strong individuality of Stone's Lady Carey (pl. 147). The sculptor, Thomas Banks, was a student at the Royal Academy when its first president, Sir Joshua Reynolds, was encouraging the heresy that realism in sculpture was 'a prostitution of a noble art' which should instead be based on the ideal and on imitation of the Antique. The figure, one of Banks's most admired works, was exhibited in 1793 at Somerset House, where

Queen Charlotte and her daughter saw it and were moved to tears.

On the base is inscribed: 'She was in form and intellect most exquisite. The unfortunate Parents ventured their all on this frail Bark, and the Wreck was total.' The Italian epitaph laments, 'She who showed us heaven earth now conceals.' In the gloom of the Boothby Chapel behind her lie her fifteenth- and sixteenth-century ancestors.

A Georgian 'auditory' church, on the eve of the Victorian reforms in liturgy and furnishings (see pp. 163, 213). The interior is dominated by the Royal Arms over the chancel arch and by a huge three-decker pulpit; from its top, the rector preaches the sermon, while in descending order below him the curate and clerk keep an eye on the congregation. Note the galleries, high box pews, people seated facing away from the east, and font used to hold the worshippers' hats. (From 'The Deformation and the Reformation', a collection of drawings of religious practices before and after their 'reformation' by the Ecclesiologists, published by Mowbray in Oxford in the mid nineteenth century.)

137 *St Mary, Croscombe, Somerset, looking east*

138, 139 St Mary, Leighton Bromswold, Huntingdonshire: west front and view across the transept

140　St Mary, Bromfield, Shropshire:
chancel ceiling

141　St John the Baptist, Halifax,
Yorkshire: window in the south choir
aisle

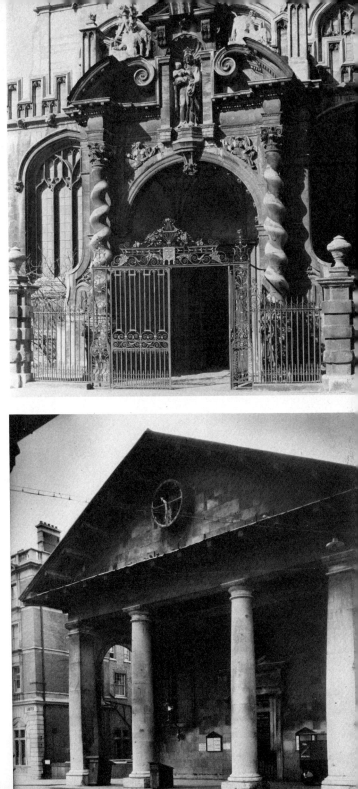

142 St Mary, Oxford: south
porch

143 St Paul, Covent Garden,
London

144 St Mary, Harefield, Middlesex: monuments of Alice Spencer, Countess of Derby, and Sophia, Lady Newdigate

(Facing page, clockwise from top left)

145 St Peter and St Paul, Borden, Kent: wall monument of Robert Plot

146 Great Brington, Northamptonshire: monument of Sir Edward Spencer

147 St Michael, Stowe-Nine-Churches, Northamptonshire: monument of Elizabeth, Lady Carey

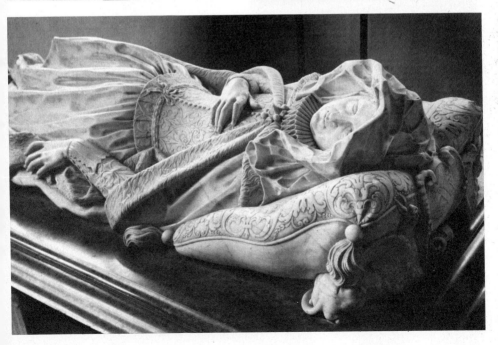

148 (left) St Mary le Bow, London

149 (below) St Vedast, Foster Lane, London

150 St James Garlickhythe, London

151 (below) St George, Bloomsbury, London

152 (right) St Michael Cornhill, London, from the south

153 St Mary Woolnoth, London

154 *St John, Smith Square, London, seen from Lord North Street*

155 *(opposite) Christ Church, Spitalfields, London*

156 (opposite) St Mary, Ingestre, Staffordshire, looking east

157 (above) St Magnus the Martyr, London, looking south-east

158 (opposite) St Stephen Walbrook,
London: view from the chancel to the
north transept

159 (right) St Clement, Eastcheap,
London: font and pulpit

160 Holy Cross and St Mary, Quainton,
Buckinghamshire: monument of Richard
and Anne Winwood

161 (opposite, above) St Mary Aldermary, London: nave and aisle vaults
162 (far left) St Margaret Pattens, London: Stuart Arms and organ
163 (left) All Hallows, Barking-by-the-Tower, London: font-cover
164 (above) St Mary at Hill, London, looking south-west

165 (*opposite*) *St Martin in the Fields, London*

166 (*below*) *St Lawrence, Mereworth, Kent*

167 (*above right*) *St Bartholomew, Tardebigge, Worcestershire, from the south-east*

168 (*right*) *St Mary le Strand, London*

169 (opposite, above) St Mary, Leebotwood, Shropshire, looking east
170 (opposite) St Mary, Whitby, Yorkshire, looking south-east
171 (above) All Saints, Petersham, Surrey, looking east

172 St Michael, Great Witley, Worcestershire: monument of the first Lord Foley, in the transept

173 Holy Cross and St Mary, Quainton, Buckinghamshire: monument of Mr Justice Dormer

174 *All Hallows, London Wall, London: chancel*

175 *(opposite) St John the Evangelist, Shobdon, Herefordshire, looking west*

176, 179 (left and opposite) St Mary Magdalene, Croome d'Abitot, Worcestershire: interior, looking west, and view from the south-west

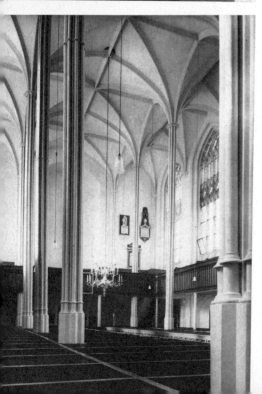

177 (above) St John the Evangelist, Shobdon, Herefordshire: Bateman Pew

178 (left) St Mary, Tetbury, Gloucestershire, looking north-west

LEI·CHE'L·CIEL·NE·MOSTRA·TERRA·N'ASCONDE·

CHAPTER SIX

After 1800:
the churches of urban and suburban England

ABOUT HALF OF ENGLAND'S PARISH CHURCHES still in use were built after 1815. This reflects the revolutionary change in English society, ways of life, and population distribution which took place between the Battle of Waterloo and the end of the last century: a change unprecedented in its scope and effects, the latter still working themselves out today.

The real Industrial Revolution did not make itself felt until after Waterloo, but thereafter its pace was swift. England by 1850 had more than doubled its population, from some 8½ to over 17 millions. But far more revolutionary was the trek to the towns from the countryside: the England of the 1851 census was already predominantly urban, with big industrial and commercial cities spreading outward into suburban communities. In 1815 London was the only city in England with more than 100,000 inhabitants; by 1900 there were over fifty such cities. Industries and foreign trade were stimulated by new canals and railways; new inventions were applied with zeal; new housing estates, the wonder of Europe and America, grew up, with water-closets for the inhabitants (even if shared); after the repeal of the Corn Laws in the 'hungry forties' food prices fell as urban employment rose; and from 1850 onwards came a spate of political, social and other reforms improving public health and longevity. When Victoria died in 1901 the population of England and Wales was 32½ millions, and the average expectation of life for both sexes, compared with 1800, had nearly doubled.

The predominantly classical style of church-building of the seventeenth and eighteenth centuries never completely obliterated the Gothic manner. Here and there churches continued to be built, unfashionably, on the older English patterns. And as the eighteenth century unfolded – as we have seen – an aristocratic, secular, Romantic movement led to a revival of interest in the Gothic style. The result was an unprecedented stylistic eclecticism. After the formation of the Church Building Society and the Church Building Act of 1818, 214 new churches were built to provide for England's growing urban population. They range from the Greek parish church of St Pancras, Euston Road (built by the Inwoods, father and son, in *184* 1819–22) to Smirke's St Mary's, Wyndham Place (where a circular tower consorts with a classical design) and Barry's Perpendicular Gothic St Peter's, Brighton. *185*

After 1815 the social and economic problems of peace racked the new urban populations (and their magistrates), and the equally new employers and their

211

families looked to the Church as a stabilizing social influence. But there were too few churches in these new urban areas, and too many for the relatively dwindling population in the countryside. In 1818 it was calculated that 2½ million people in the new industrial areas were without church-room.

At the time of the Reform Bill of 1832 the Church was so unpopular that it was assumed it would soon be disestablished. Cartoons of the 1830s represent bishops, deans, prebendaries and country parsons as fat, worldly and rapacious, battening on the poor. 'The Church as it now is no human power can save', wrote Dr Arnold, headmaster of Rugby. But the danger was averted by the reform of the hated tithe system and by changes in the distribution of clerical wealth. Tithes were commuted for a rent-charge on land, which was eventually paid by the landowner and not by the tenant farmer. And the gap between rich and poor clergy, forcefully portrayed in Trollope's 'Barsetshire' novels, was partially bridged. Taxes could no longer be raised for church-building and the Church had to rely on voluntary subscriptions, as the Free Churches had always had to do. Individual generosity provided the money for many new churches. St Stephen, Rochester Row, London was built by Benjamin Ferrey at the expense of Baroness *189–* Burdett Coutts and Street's St James the Less, Pimlico was financed by the Misses *191* Monk as a memorial to their father, the late Bishop of Gloucester. It was characteristic of the period that political and social differences should take on a markedly religious flavour. The keenest Anglicans in both urban and rural areas were Conservatives, while the Dissenters were Whigs and Liberals. Englishmen were not so much class conscious as conscious of Church versus Chapel, a situation brilliantly depicted by George Eliot in the opening chapters of *Felix Holt*.

The true Gothic Revival in church architecture began within the Church with demands for a return to the old *Ecclesia Anglicana* and her ritual, vestments, altars, mysteries and pervasive sense of holiness. These demands came from two sources. The first was the Tractarian ('Oxford') Movement, centred in Oxford where it was sparked off by John Keble's Assize sermon in 1833 referring to 'national apostasy'. It was popular among many younger priests, including John Henry Newman, who eventually turned to Roman Catholicism. The second Anglican impetus for the Gothic Revival came from the Cambridge undergraduate Camden Society, under the leadership of J. M. Neale and Benjamin Webb, which aimed to reform and restore the architecture, layout and ritual of English churches. They were inspired in this by the polemical fervour of the young Augustus Welby Northmore Pugin, a Catholic convert, who in 1836 published *Contrasts*, a witty and impassioned plea in words and pictures for a return from the ugly, materialistic world of his day to the noble, beautiful, and eminently Christian Middle Ages. The objects and activities of the Cambridge Camden Society were summed up by a new word, 'Ecclesiology', which was defined by A. J. B. Beresford Hope, one of the founder members, as 'the science of worship carried out in all its material development'. With its influential (and impressive) periodical *The Ecclesiologist*, started in 1841, and its distinguished patrons who included archbishops, bishops, peers and members of Parliament, the Cambridge Camden Society came to exercise an almost tyrannical authority over parish church-building.

The starting point of the Ecclesiologists was the belief that there was a specifically Christian style of architecture in which every church should be built. That style was thirteenth-century Gothic. And there was also a definite plan to which a church intended for Prayer Book worship must conform. That plan, so they thought, had also reached perfection in the thirteenth century. They imagined that the various features of medieval buildings were all symbolic and overlooked the fact that they had also been designed to meet practical needs. Thus, without considering the question of the congregation's convenience the Ecclesiologists laid down that a church should consist of a sanctuary, a spacious chancel and a nave, together symbolizing the Trinity.

In their attempt to make architecture conform to what they thought to be true symbolism the Ecclesiologists did much harm to old parish churches. Gilbert Scott in his *Plea for the Faithful Restoration of our Ancient Churches* gives a horrifying picture of the destructive restorers who pulled down medieval survivals of the 'wrong' period and rebuilt them in the 'best' Gothic style. At the same time, however, there were some conservative restorers who retained all that remained of medieval work, replacing what was missing with scholarly replicas. The churches of Holkham in Norfolk and Ickleton in Cambridgeshire are instances of the two approaches. The original character of the former is almost totally obscured by the hard, insensitive rebuilding by James Colling, while the remarkable interior of Ickleton was, except for the chancel, respected by the Victorian restorers, who even replaced those fleuron-bordered bench-ends destroyed during the Civil War with careful copies of the few that survived.

The tenets of the Ecclesiologists were of course entirely opposed to the arrangement in an auditory church. High pews were condemned not only because *169,* they were conducive to irreverence but because they often prevented the *180* congregation from seeing the altar and from praying towards it. Pews were to be low, and all were to face the east end. The altar was to be raised on steps; and the *189,* chancel, especially if there were no screen, was to be raised two or three steps above *191* the level of the nave. This accounts for the array of shining new tiles, generally brown and wasp yellow, red or dark blue, in the chancel and sanctuaries of restored medieval as well as Victorian churches. It also recognizes the most important fact – that the altar is the focus of devotion for every Church of England service.

The Ecclesiologists particularly detested the three-storeyed pulpit. In *A Few Words to Church Builders* Neale denounced it as both hideous aesthetically and 'repugnant to all Catholic principles of devotion'. He urged that the minister should read the lessons from a lectern placed in the nave on one side of the chancel and opposite the pulpit. The eagle lectern, such a conspicuous item of furniture in *191* many churches, was the type recommended.

The most important contribution of the Oxford Tractarians to the setting of Anglican worship was the surpliced choir occupying stalls in the chancel. Dr W. F. Hook, vicar of Leeds, was instrumental in the rebuilding of his church to conform to the new principles. Hook's friend Dr John Jebb was passionately interested in cathedral choirs and encouraged him to introduce a choir into his new church to sing Matins and Evensong daily. The 'white-robed company of men and boys stationed at each side of the chancel . . . daily ministering the service of prayer and thanksgiving' became the model for choirs in all parish churches.

A further alteration in the arrangement of church furnishing was the placing of
192   the organ in or near the chancel so that it was close to the choir. It still occupies this uncomely position in many parish churches.

The efforts of what began as a small society of undergraduates had extraordinary results. One was that in an age when faith was being steadily eroded by scientific discovery almost every architect of note was occupied to a considerable extent with work on churches. They designed not only the buildings but also the furnishings, and in this they were supported by several major manufacturers who specialized in church fittings and ornaments, notably John Hardman and Co., stained glass and metal workers, Clayton and Bell, stained glass workers, John Keith and Son, manufacturers of plate, and Rattee and Kett of Cambridge, woodworkers.

It is not possible here to mention more than a few of the enormous number of churches built in the Gothic style after about 1845. Butterfield, Carpenter, Pearson, Ferrey, Brooks, Street, Bodley (through whom William Morris's firm of Morris, Marshall, Faulkner and Co., founded in 1861, received most of their ecclesiastical commissions), Cundy, Scott, J.F. Bentley (a Catholic, whose rare Anglican work included St Luke's, Chiddingstone Causeway, Kent), Blore, Seddon, the three Seddings, Teulon and Waterhouse all designed Gothic parish churches. Even Burges, whose interests were primarily in domestic architecture, but who, together with Butterfield and Street, was closely associated with the Ecclesiological Society as a designer of church furnishing and plate, made his own striking contribution in the vital, solid and opulent churches of Studley Royal and Skelton, Yorkshire, and the fine bulk of St Faith's, Stoke Newington, London.

One noble monument to all this activity must be mentioned – Butterfield's All Saints, Margaret Street, just off London's Oxford Street, completed in 1859. It was the epitome of all the striving of Ecclesiologists and Tractarians, rendered into many-coloured brick, granite, marble and Cornish alabaster, tiles, stained glass and gilding. One has only to walk about in it to see the passionate concern with details, colours and effects (vertical and horizontal, two-dimensional and more) of all of its fashioners. The awkward site was utilized to produce mysterious or aesthetic effects by structural (strictly English Gothic) devices or even incongruities, affording unusual perspectives or contrasting views. 'Having done this,' wrote Ruskin of it, 'we may do anything.' Butterfield's stern and uncompromising character (there were no lunch-breaks in his office) even appears in relatively small
195   compositions, such as the font at Ottery St Mary.

After the international competition held in 1855 for the design of a cathedral at Lille – which had to be in the French Gothic style – new influences affected English church-building and architects began to abandon the 'national' style. Bodley remained true to the Ecclesiologists' ideals (though not to their fourteenth-century Gothic) in his church of the Holy Angels at Hoar Cross, Staffordshire, with its high, important chancel and sumptuous decorations, but early French Gothic had
192   always been the preference of Burges and Clutton, winners of the Lille

competition. Street's vigorous polychromatic church of St James the Less, Pimlico,   *189–*
was inspired by both French and Italian traditions. Pearson, who delighted in the   *191*
ingenious construction of elaborate vaults, based his characteristically tall churches
(of which St Augustine's, Kilburn, begun in 1871, and St Michael's, Croydon,   *198,*
begun in 1880, are the most famous) on foreign example. Seddon employed that   *199*
rare style, beloved of Ruskin, Venetian Gothic. J. D. Sedding, author of Holy
Trinity, Sloane Street (almost incredibly, now menaced with demolition), in   *203*
which he employed many other artists, including Burne-Jones, Powell, Hamo
Thornycroft, Onslow Ford, Boucher, F. W. Pomeroy and H. Starkie Gardner,   *210*
used Gothic of the fifteenth century with originality and excelled in the design of
screens, reredoses, plate and crosses. His nephew Edmund produced a most
striking variation on fifteenth-century Gothic at St Peter's, Shaldon, Devon. S. S.   *200*
Teulon resorted to flamboyant and conflicting combinations, as in St Stephen's,
Hampstead, where red and yellow brick consort with stone and segmental-headed
openings confront pointed arches.

An overwhelming example of Gothic inspiration embodied in a markedly
individual building is the church of St Bartholomew's, Brighton, designed by   *195*
Edmund Scott for a dynamic local churchman, Father Wagner, and built in
1872–74. The immensely lofty, aisleless structure is of plain brick throughout,
relieved by neither mouldings nor sculptural adornment but only by a single giant
rose window and tall clerestory openings. E. S. Prior's church at Roker Park,   *206,*
Durham (1906–07), with transverse arches and simplified tracery, is so simple that   *207*
it might have been designed for concrete rather than the far more expressive and
massive local stone. At Great Warley, Essex, by Harrison Townsend (1904), a   *204*
modest roughcast exterior reflecting the vernacular interests of the period conceals
a tunnel-vaulted, aisleless nave flaunting one of the most dazzling displays of Art
Nouveau decoration in the country, the work of Sir William Reynolds Stephens.

Pious historicism persisted in the 'correct' English Gothic of Temple Moore
(who built St Margaret's, Leeds, in 1908 and St Mary's, Hendon, in 1914). As late as
1935 the pale purple exterior of St Catherine, Mile Cross, Norwich, by A. D.   *205*
Caroë and A. P. Robinson, still vaguely evoked the mighty forms of Norman
architecture.

As the twentieth century wore on, with two world wars, the problems of the
Church of England multiplied, as did those of almost all other religions in the
world. Widespread indifference was curiously combined with liturgical
dogmatism. Architecture grew more and more preoccupied with materials, bare
outlines, experimentation, the breaking of new pathways and rejection of the old.
Inter-denominational common-use buildings – chapels at universities, airports and
other public places – were designed without reference to the English past and made
increasing use of pre-fabricated parts. Many parish and other churches built since
1945 seem to proclaim their (perhaps very temporary) contemporaneity, both in
design and furnishings. Examples include St Paul's, Bow Common, Stepney by
Robert Maguire and Keith Murray, St George's, Farnham Royal, Buckinghamshire by H. Braddock and D. Martin-Smith, and Sir Basil Spence's St Catherine's,
Woodthorpe, Yorkshire.

Two paradoxical movements over the last 150 years have led to the present problems of the Church of England and its parishes. First, the migration from the country to the towns depopulated the villages and left huge, old, historic churches in over-supply and under-maintained; secondly, the nineteenth-century wave of church-building in the new urban and suburban areas endowed cities with parishes and churches which are themselves now superfluous, equally ill-attended and ill-served and ill-maintained, as city centres are neglected.

We owe to the great Victorian and Neo-Georgian architects the preservation of many of our older historic parish churches, as well as the destruction of a few and the over-restoration of others. To the Gothic Revival architects we also owe a remarkable collection of new churches. But today, as the whirligig of Time brings his revenges we witness once again the old enemies at work: outright demolition or slow decay, among both the historic and the not-so-historic parish churches of England, in an era of popular disbelief unparalleled since 1,500 years ago 'the English gat hold of the land'.

Yet authorities have but to threaten one historic church with demolition and a popular movement for its retention immediately arises. Deep down among the English is a feeling that what Wulfstan of Worcester called the 'heaping up of stones' for churches through thirteen centuries ought not to be lost, ruined.

Notes on the plates

183 Swaffham, Norfolk: churchyard memorial to Susan Blythe
The full-length angels who occasionally appear on seventeenth-and eighteenth-century tombstones are generally robust creatures sounding the trump of doom and associating with images of death and decay rather than future bliss. These Swaffham angels of 1854, clad in Victorian night-gowns instead of the ample skirts or feathered tights of earlier periods, reflect a significant change from symbolism to sentimentality. Like the angels of Burne-Jones, who said he would paint more and more of them the more materialistic the world became, they represent an escape from disturbing truths, an evasion of reality. They remind us of the conflicting, para-doxical attitudes that underlie and impair even the finest of the buildings at which we are going to look.

184 St Pancras, London: view from the south-east
Built between 1819 and 1822 to supplement the tiny Norman parish church, New St Pancras was the first Greek Revival church in London. In designing it William Inwood had the help of his much more brilliant son, Henry William, who had just returned from Greece, and the tower – though it lodges like an afterthought on the roof of a classical temple, as at St Martin in the Fields (pl. 165) – is modelled on the Tower of the Winds at Athens. The Ionic portico on the front follows that of the Erechtheion, and on either side of the east end jut copies of the Erechtheion's caryatid portico. The figures, modelled in terracotta on cast-iron cores, serve as guardians of the burial vaults, entered by the door below them.

185 St Peter, Brighton, Sussex
186 St Luke, Chelsea, London
187 St Michael, Highgate, London
188 St Andrew, Ombersley, Worcestershire: interior, looking west
These four churches illustrate the freedom with which Gothic was interpreted at the time of the Church Building Act of 1818, before the Ecclesiologists had established standards of correctness (pp. 212–213).

Sir Charles Barry's St Peter, Brighton (1824–28), has all the charm of eighteenth-century Gothick combined with architectural originality and solidity. The contrast in proportion between the recessed slender upper stages of the tower and the broad ground storey, the resemblances in ornamental detail, the huge ogival openings, the pretty, pierced parapets and the narrow, richly pinnacled aisles, make an impression of zest and brilliance which is not dimmed either by the wizardry of Nash's great folly nearby or the glitter of the billowing Regency terraces.

The open, ogee-arched porch spread across the whole front of St Luke, Chelsea, built by James Savage in 1820–24, has a playful Georgian air about it, but this church is always considered to be the product of a more serious study of medieval architecture, since it is vaulted in stone instead of plaster.

Lewis Vulliamy's tall, preternaturally thin, aspiring brick and ashlar west end of St Michael, Highgate (1830), reveals a similar predilection for Gothick ogival forms and just a touch of individual fantasy in the oddly canted, turreted and gabled angles of the aisles.

The architect of St Andrew, Ombersley (1825–29), was Thomas Rickman, author of *Attempts to Discriminate the Styles of English Architecture* (1819) and originator of the terms by which the various medieval styles are known. But despite his scholarly interest, this interior has a slim elegance and a plaster vault which relate it to Hiorn's eighteenth-century interior at Tetbury (pl. 178). The previous century is also vividly recalled by the box pews and the gallery, which form an unusually complete ensemble. The church was built in the grounds of the lord of the manor, Lord Sandys, and the throne-like squire's pew against the chancel arch is conspicuous.

189–191 St James the Less, Thorndike Street, London: view towards the chancel, capital and furnishings
St James the Less, like St Barnabas (pl. 193), was intended as an inspiration to the slum dwellers of Pimlico. George Edmund Street built it in 1858–61 for the Misses Monk, who provided the £5,000 that it cost as a memorial to their father, late Bishop of Gloucester. Street had lately returned from an extensive tour of Spain, France, Germany and Italy and his church reflects some of his experiences, transformed by one of the most masterful imaginations of the age. The photographs convey the amazing strength, the mass and compelling detail of this remarkable building. The chancel is the focus of the interior, in accordance with the strict Tractarian principles which Street, an Oxford man and sincere Christian, supported.

The church is of red brick varied with bands of darker brick – even the ribbed vault of the choir and sanctuary is carried out in this material – and the glowing red colour, accentuated by the deliberately archaic glass paintings by Clayton and Bell, pervades the dark interior. The mystery is intensified by cleverly contrived vistas, glimpses of side chapels and by strange, disturbing proportions: high vaults and towering arches of cut brick set on excessively short stout columns of polished red granite.

Nave and chancel are separated by a very low stone and wrought-iron screen, and the sanctuary is enclosed by walls of inlaid marble incorporating the curved reredos. Between the chancel and north chapel are further screens of wrought iron, on top of which can be seen some of Street's novel gas fittings, now no longer used. The polished brass lectern is in the traditional form of an eagle (see pl. 82). The pulpit, its strong and heavy forms characteristic of Street, was carved by Earp, and Watts painted the fresco of Christ in Majesty over the chancel arch. The capitals, combining varieties of stiff-leaf foliage with monsters, angels and representations of the parables, were carved by Thomas Farmer.

Street was the original inspiration of the Arts and Crafts Movement: Philip Webb started out as his assistant and William Morris was for a time his pupil. He was concerned with every detail of the fabric and furnishing, from the leaves and flowers of the metalwork to the stencilled designs on the yellow Mansfield stone.

192 St Mary, Woburn, Bedfordshire, looking east from the entrance
Henry Clutton's church is a splendidly clear, vigorous and convinced version of his preferred style, early French Gothic. It was built in 1864–68 for the eighth Duke of Bedford, who spared no expense, and the fine Bath stone of the fabric, which extends to the vaults, contributes greatly to its success. The design is unusual in having aisles almost as high as the nave.

193 St Barnabas, Pimlico, London: nave and font-cover
The church was built in 1846–48 by Thomas Cundy, largely with money raised in response to an appeal by the Rev. W. Bennett (the first incumbent) for a place of worship which would provide an edifying contrast to 'the dens of infamy and the haunts of vice, ignorance, filth and atheism' of the only recently developed district. Cundy chose the Early English style as 'best suited for a poor man's church'. The *Ecclesiologist* (see p. 212) took exception, arguing that 'of all men, he whose dwelling is mean and poor, has the greatest claim to richness and magnificence in the temple of the Lord'. It was pleased to find the furnishings not only correct but sumptuous. They soon became notorious, associated with ritualist practices which brought the Rev. Bennett into violent controversy. Attendance at St Barnabas involved defiance of convention, and far from

attracting the inmates of Pimlico's slums, the church appealed particularly to the younger aristocracy of Belgravia, who compared its atmosphere with that of such recently published poems of Tennyson as *The Lady of Shalott*.

Cundy was assisted by the young Butterfield (see pls. 195, 197), and the font of Purbeck marble with its wooden cover, more like a miniature baptistery, heralds the strenuous individuality of the 1860s and 1870s.

194 St Mary Abbot, Kensington, London: font
The interior of this church, rebuilt by Sir George Gilbert Scott in 1869-72, too unfeelingly counterfeits an Early English setting to kindle an energetic response, but the marble font with its ceremonial metal cover instantly attracts attention. The bowl is an interesting variation on an Early English model (compare pl. 9), and its solidity is emphasized by the airy geometric patterns described by the wrought-iron cover. This was made by the Skidmore Art Manufactures Company of Coventry, who carried out most of Scott's metalwork designs, including the great choir screens at Lichfield and (formerly) Hereford and Salisbury.

195 St Mary, Ottery St Mary, Devon: font
The impression of imperious, assertive originality made by Butterfield's chancel at Babbacombe (pl. 197) is reinforced by this eccentric font of 1850 which so conspicuously contrasts with its medieval surroundings. It not only shows Butterfield's love of bright, patterned colour but his interest in local materials, which he exploited more than any builder of the Gothic period. All the marbles of which this piece is made are from Devon and Cornwall, with the exception of the white, which came from Sicily. The arcaded cover, with its projections like bishops' thrones and an extraordinary metal crowning feature, sits on the square basin and stumpy Byzantine columns with disconcerting authority.

196 St Bartholomew, Brighton, Sussex: interior, looking west
197 All Saints, Babbacombe, Devon: chancel
These radically different interiors were both

completed in 1874. St Bartholomew is conspicuous among its contemporaries for an architectural grandeur which can be enjoyed without reminders of the failure in sentiment which nearly always attended the reproduction of medieval forms in a materialistic society. The Gothic embraced by its architect, the little-known, local Edmund Scott, is not historical: an Italianate use of brick, lofty arched recesses with triple lancet openings above each and gigantic clerestory windows echoing their shape, a high wagon roof with tie-beams – higher than the nave of Westminster Abbey – and a colossal, plain rose window to the west conspire to create an austere interior which without exaggeration can be called sublime. It was paid for by Father Arthur Wagner, who presented four other churches as well to the poorer areas of Brighton.

Butterfield's church at Babbacombe (1865-74), as richly ornate as St Bartholomew's is bare, expresses the same individuality in the organization of spatial effects. It also shows the addiction to applied decoration and 'constructional poly-chromy' which had earlier distinguished Butterfield's London church of All Saints, Margaret Street (see p. 214) and such work as his font at Ottery St Mary (pl. 195). The display of coloured marbles, alabaster, tiles, stencilled sprays, incised patterns filled with painted mastic, and glittering metalwork, would be entirely daunting were it not for the muted colours of the chancel, sea-green, ochre, light and dark grey and rose, colours which throw into relief the restless structural lines and shapes and the giant cusped window-like arch into the chancel aisle. This interior and its furnishings, also designed by Butterfield, play upon medieval motifs with a panache which goes far beyond archaeological medievalism.

198, 199 St Augustine, Kilburn, London: west front, and interior, looking towards the chancel and south transept
One of the most ambitious and original of all Victorian churches, St Augustine was designed by John Loughborough Pearson in 1870 and was substantially complete by 1877, though the immense spire (254 feet high) that soars above the west front with its deeply recessed wheel window was not finished until 1898. The interior view, taken

from the gallery which runs so un-expectedly above the arcade and bridges the transepts, emphasizes the height and mys-terious vistas of this unique arrangement of space. From this vantage-point the vast gallery openings and the lofty ribbed vaults (a speciality of Pearson) make their full dizzy impact. The division between the severe nave and ornate choir is marked not by any narrowing or change in roof-line but by a high stone rood-screen. The painted decoration on the brick walls was done by Clayton and Bell.

200 St Peter, Shaldon, Teignmouth, Devon: nave, seen through the chancel screen
The architect of this striking church (1893–1902), the younger Edmund Sed-ding, was the nephew of J.D. Sedding, designer of Holy Trinity, Sloane Street (pl. 203, opposite), and shared his uncle's preference for the inspiration of nature and his urge to break away from strict confor-mity to the Gothic style. Indeed J.D. Sedding's belief that the artist could 'entice the soul of the tangled thicket into the mazes of his carved and beaten work' and 'bring the might of tall cliffs into his walls' is given concrete form in the screen of St Peter, with its virile, thorny, briar-like aspect, and in the craggy arcades. The barrel vault gives a surprising twist to a local style (see pl. 115) by translating it into stone.

201 St Protus and St Hyacinth, Blisland, Cornwall: rood-screen
The screen was designed by Frederic Charles Eden, an assistant of Bodley better known for his glass, embroidery and fittings than for his buildings, and made by local workmen in 1896. It is part of Eden's restoration of the church and is an instance of a medieval building actually gaining in visual delight by a Victorian addition. While it preserves some traditional features (compare pl. 108), the screen is frankly of its own time. Its rich, glowing colours – gold, green, white and red – emphasize the simplicity of this rural nave with its local slate floor and alarmingly un-perpendicular Perpendicular piers.

202 St Cyprian, Clarence Gate, London: rood-screen
The golden screen, extending right across

the nave and aisles in the medieval West Country manner which its style also emulates (pl. 108), is the most prominent object in Sir Ninian Comper's white interior. After the bold, idiosyncratic Gothic of Street and Butterfield (pls. 189, 197), this exquisite pastiche, created in 1903, astonishes by its detailed delicacy. The close reproduction of medieval work, allied to such unmistakably period features as the Burne-Jonesian angels standing on wheels and the contrast between white and gold, betrays a further retreat from the present than any of the more aggressive Gothic creations of the High Victorians. The masquerade at St Cyprian's went so far at the consecration ceremony, thronged by rich, admiring Edwardians, that the floor was strewn with flowers and rushes in the medieval manner and the service followed the ancient Pontifical of Egbert, the eighth-century Bishop of York.

203 Holy Trinity, Sloane Street, London: detail of the nave wall
John Dando Sedding was a pupil of G.E. Street and a leader of the Arts and Crafts Movement, in strong reaction against nineteenth-century mass production and materialism. He was not only an architect but a designer of metalwork, embroidery and wallpapers, in all of which natural ornament plays a prominent part (see the note to pl. 200). At Holy Trinity it is the detail and ornament, carried out by master craftsmen (see p. 215 and pl. 210), which chiefly arouse interest, although Sedding's free interpretation of Perpendicular gives pleasure, especially the arcade spandrel ornaments of flat medallions and miniature Gothic windows laid on their sides. The church was whitewashed in 1930 on the ad-vice of F.C. Eden (see pl. 201), so the furnishings can no longer be seen against the dull gold colour Sedding chose to set them off. The wrought-iron electric light fittings, instinct with feeling for growing forms, but not at all Gothic, were designed by Sedding himself and the pretty corbel putti were the work of Henry Wilson, sculptor and metalworker and Sedding's chief assistant.

204 St Mary the Virgin, Great Warley, Essex: chancel and pulpit
It is the choice and use of materials that

makes the interior of Great Warley a memorable experience. The church was built in 1904 by Harrison Townsend and decorated by the American-born Sir William Reynolds Stephens, a follower of the sculptor Sir Alfred Gilbert (creator of the Eros fountain at Piccadilly). It is a dazzling riot of Art Nouveau design. The chancel apse is sheathed in palest green marble below a stylized grape design in aluminium, very much a metal of the period. The figure of Christ above the altar is of copper, faced with oxydized silver; He tramples on a serpent, symbol of death. The choir screen is formed of dark green Irish marble from which grow blossoming trees, signifying resurrection and life, among whose leaves are fruits of red glass, flowers of shell, and angels of oxydized silver. The pulpit in the foreground is of hammered copper inset with coloured enamels.

205 St Catherine, Mile Cross, Norwich, Norfolk: interior, looking east
Built by A. D. Caroë and A. P. Robinson in 1935, the design avoids actual medieval detail in an evocation of vaguely Norman massiveness. However, the fashionable use of concrete in the interior robs it of the sense of locality (expressed by its brick exterior) which could have given life to the plain surfaces.

206, 207 St Andrew, Roker Park, Co. Durham: interior, looking west, and view from the east
St Andrew at Roker diverges from medieval tradition without actually breaking with it. Its architect, E. S. Prior, was a pupil of Norman Shaw and one of the founders of the Art Workers' Guild and the Arts and Crafts Exhibition Society. It was natural that he should care deeply about materials. The effectiveness of his austere church of 1906–07 depends largely on the rough grey local stone of which it is built and which harmonizes with the eccentrically simplified, suggestive rather than imitation Gothic of the style. The enormous transverse arches rest on squat, polygonal piers, creating low narrow passages rather than aisles. Window tracery is merely adumbrated by match-stick, criss-cross patterns. The furnishing was a matter of importance to Prior. The chancel carpet was woven

from a design by William Morris and the choir stalls, pulpit and lectern were designed by Ernest Gimson (see pl. 209).

208 St Andrew, Mells, Somerset: memorial to Mrs Alfred Lyttelton
The peacock on this coloured gesso relief, designed by Burne-Jones in 1886, is as much a trademark of the Aesthetic Movement as the sunflower. The pillars of the sarcophagus and the lettering it bears reflect the growing interest in Byzantine and Early Medieval art which provided an alternative to Gothic in the late nineteenth century. Mrs Lyttelton's sister, Mrs Horner, was lady of the manor and a friend of the artist.

209 St Andrew, Roker Park, Co. Durham: lectern
One of the furnishings specially commissioned by Prior from Ernest Gimson (see pl. 206) is the lectern, suitably simple in shape but finely inlaid with mother-of-pearl, silver, ebony and ivory. The candlesticks are of polished wrought iron. Gimson, a pupil of J. D. Sedding and himself a great craftsman, was one of the outstanding figures in the Arts and Crafts Movement, and characteristically chose the rural Cotswolds as a setting for his workshop.

210 Holy Trinity, Sloane Street, London: detail of the choir stalls
The coiling, intricate forms, the windswept foliage and lethargic figures of F. W. Pomeroy's beaten and cast bronze panels decorating the choir stalls at Holy Trinity resemble the designs of William Morris and Walter Crane. The central figure is, appropriately for choir stalls, King David.

211 St Cuthbert, Philbeach Gardens, London: chancel and lectern
This Tractarian church, built by A. D. Gough in 1884, is celebrated for its furnishings, typical of the Arts and Crafts Movement, by William Bainbridge Reynolds, who was a pupil of Street before joining the metalworking shop of Starkie Gardner. Reynolds designed and made the communion rails, the lectern, the pulpit and the bridge-like rood-beam on which there was originally a small altar with a tabernacle for the reservation of the consecrated

elements. The towering, crowded reredos of wood was carved by the architect-clergyman, the Rev. Ernest Geldart.

The great branching lectern, crowned by the figure of St John the Baptist, is one of Bainbridge Reynolds's finest pieces, though it was the first of his commissioned works, designed in 1885. It is of wrought iron and repoussé copper with enamel decoration in the swirling ribbon ornament. The enamel work was done by Nelson Dawson, art director of the Artificers' Guild of which he was a founder, and Clement Heaton. The two sides of the lectern, fantastically draped with ribbons of copper, were intended for the Old Testament, bound in copper, and the New Testament, bound in silver.

212 St Michael, Great Tew, Oxfordshire: monument of Mary Anne Boulton
Carved in 1834, before Victoria came to the throne, by Sir Francis Chantrey, who was himself dead by 1841, this portrait effigy breathes an air of Victorian piety, reinforced by the words inscribed on the open marble book – which were to be repeated on countless nineteenth-century tombstones – and reveals a vein of softness and sentimentality which suitably brings this final chapter to a close.

184 St Pancras, London, from the south-east

185 (left) St Peter, Brighton, Sussex

187 (below) St Michael, Highgate, London

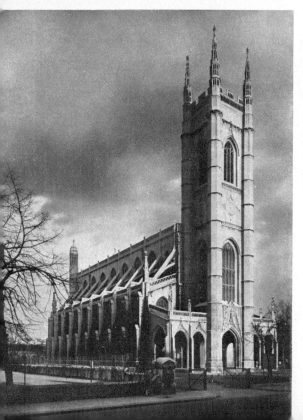

186 (left) St Luke, Chelsea, London

188 (opposite) St Andrew, Ombersley, Worcestershire, looking west

189–191 *St James the Less,*
Thorndike Street, London:
view towards the chancel,
capital and furnishings

192 (opposite) St Mary, Woburn, Bedfordshire, looking east from the entrance

193 (right) St Barnabas, Pimlico, London: nave and font-cover

194 (above) St Mary Abbot, Kensington, London: font

195 (right) St Mary, Ottery St Mary, Devon: font

96 (opposite) *St Bartholomew, Brighton, Sussex, looking west*

97 (above) *All Saints, Babbacombe, Devon: chancel*

198, 199 St Augustine, Kilburn, London: west front, and view towards the chancel and south transept

200 *(left) St Peter, Shaldon,
Teignmouth, Devon: nave, seen through
the chancel screen*

202 *(below) St Cyprian, Clarence Gate,
London: rood-screen*

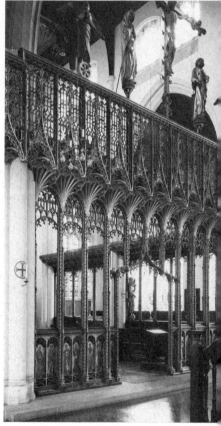

201 *(left) St Protus and St
Hyacinth, Blisland, Cornwall: rood-screen*

203 *(opposite) Holy Trinity, Sloane
Street, London: detail of the nave wall*

204 *St Mary the Virgin, Great Warley,
Essex: chancel and pulpit*

205 *St Catherine, Mile Cross, Norwich,
Norfolk, looking east*

206, 207 *(opposite) St Andrew, Roker
Park, Co. Durham: interior, looking
west, and view from the east*

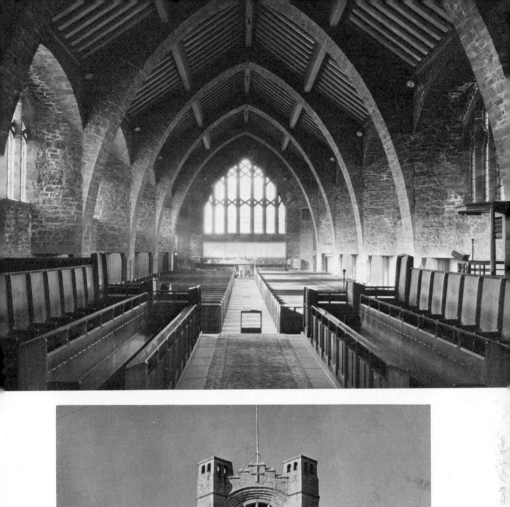

208 (left) St Andrew, Mells, Somerset: memorial to Mrs Alfred Lyttelton

209 (below) St Andrew, Roker Park, Co. Durham: lectern

210 (below) Holy Trinity, Sloane Street, London: choir stalls

211 (opposite) St Cuthbert, Philbeach Gardens, London

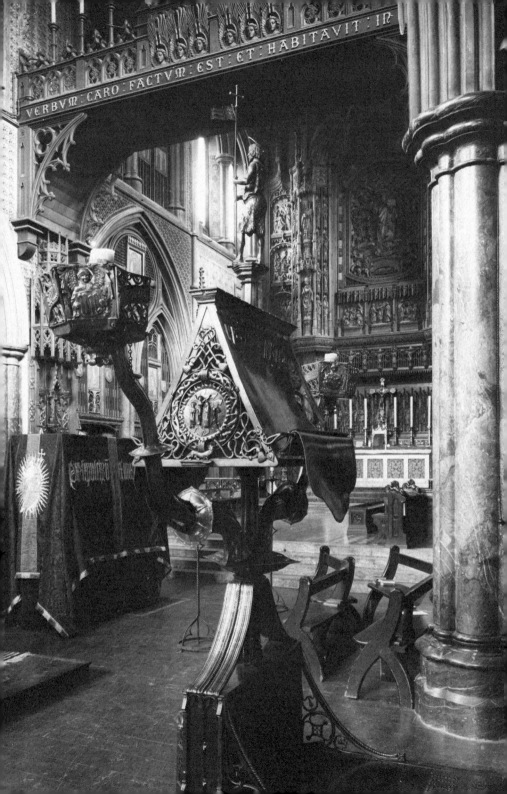

Church plans
Glossary
Select bibliography
List of places, by counties
Index

212 St Michael, Great Tew, Oxfordshire: *monument of Mary Anne Boulton*

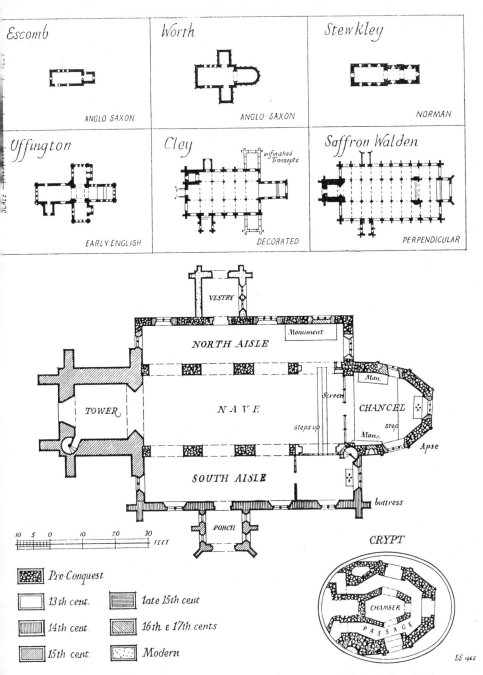

The evolution of church plans, shown in six separate buildings, each typical of its period, and in the church at Wing, Buckinghamshire, a remarkable Anglo-Saxon structure altered through the centuries. (Drawn by Edwin Smith)

Glossary

ABACUS: A slab at the top of a capital, like a cap or crown over it.

AISLE: Literally 'wing'; the sideways extension of the nave.

APSE: Rounded or polygonal end – generally eastern – of a church, transept or chapel.

ASHLAR: Masonry or squared stones in regular courses.

BAY: Compartment(s) dividing the nave or roof of a building. Also a projecting window.

BUTTRESS: Masonry built against a wall to strengthen it, or to resist the outward thrust of an arch or vault from above. (See FLYING BUTTRESS.)

CAPITAL: Topmost portion of a column or pier, or of a whole group of columns and piers.

CHANCEL: The holy place where the altar is situated, behind the 'bar' or rails.

CHANTRY: Place (e.g. chapel) where prayers were to be said for the soul of the founder(s) who had left a fund for that purpose.

CHOIR: Part of church for the use of singers, generally between nave and chancel and separated from the nave by rail or screen.

CLERESTORY: Upper part of nave wall, containing windows, generally above the aisle roofs.

CLUNCH: A soft, white limestone.

COPING: The capping or covering along the top of a wall.

CORBEL: A bracket, often elaborately carved or moulded, projecting from a wall to support the beams of a roof, the ribs of a vault, or a statue.

CORNICE: A projection round or along the top of buildings or rooms. In Classical or Renaissance buildings, it is the upper part of the entablature.

COURSE: A continuous line of stones, bricks, etc., evenly laid along a wall.

CROCKET: A projecting knob of a stone, carved with curving foliage, arranged in sequence along the lines of spires, canopies of tombs, gables, etc.

CROSSING: Intersection of the nave of a church with the transepts, sometimes supporting a (central) tower.

CRYPT: Literally 'secret' place; originally the underground chamber where a martyr's, then a saint's, relics rested beneath the high altar; later, any underground chamber below a church, e.g. a charnel or bone-house.

CUSP(s): The projecting points formed by the intersection of the small arcs or foils in tracery.

DRIP-COURSE: A projecting course to catch and throw off rainwater.

ENGAGED: Attached to the fabric, e.g. a pilaster.

ENTABLATURE: The entire horizontal portion resting on the columns in Classical architecture.

FOIL: Small opening, or curved 'bite', taken out of the stone or wooden members of door and window openings, or of decorative arcading. According to their grouping in threes, fours, fives, etc., they are known as trefoil, quatrefoil, cinquefoil, etc.

FLUSHWORK: Inlaid stone and flush-faced flint work, in patterns, found mainly in East Anglian flint districts.

FLYING BUTTRESS: An external arch springing over the roof of an aisle and supporting the wall of the clerestory. It is also used to support the sides of spires and lanterns, and is sometimes called an arch-buttress.

FRIEZE: The middle part of the entablature in Classical architecture.

GABLE: Triangular portion of a wall between the enclosing lines of a sloping roof.

HAMMERBEAM: A projecting beam to support a roof by 'building-up', i.e. without a direct tie-beam across.

IMPOST: Upper portion of a pier, column or pillar, usually moulded, on which an arch rests.

JAMB: The upright side-member of a door, window, etc.

KEYSTONE: The central and topmost voussoir, locking the arch. (See VOUSSOIRS.)

LIGHT(s): Distinct openings of mullioned and transomed windows.

LINTEL: The horizontal member across the top of a door.

MISERICORD: Tip-up seat in choir stalls, having a smaller support on the underside, frequently grotesquely carved, on which the user might recline yet remain, technically, 'on his feet'.

MOULDING: Contours given to any projections, generally by carving.

MULLION(S): Vertical member(s) of a window, dividing it into a number of lights.

NARTHEX: An entrance-annex before the main portal, generally in early churches, and at the west end.

NAVE: From Latin *navis*, a ship; the western and main body of the church, for ordinary folk.

PIER: A mass of masonry (as distinct from a pillar or column) from which an arch springs. Sometimes applied to the portions of a wall between doors and windows.

PILASTER: A pillar attached to (engaged in) the wall and projecting only about one-sixth of its breadth from the wall.

PISCINA: Literally 'fishpond'; a washing-and-draining stoup in a niche near the altar, generally let into the wall, for cleansing sacred vessels.

POPPYHEAD: Head of a bench, or pew-end, brought up to a carved figure or emblem.

PRESBYTERY: Eastern part of a large church, kept exclusively for the use of clergy; applied sometimes to the choir only, but often to the whole sanctuary.

QUOIN(S): Corner-stone(s) at the angles of buildings; sometimes applied to the angle itself.

REREDOS: Decorative long panel above, and sometimes all round, an altar.

ROOD: Crucifix; generally the one which stood upon the screen separating chancel from nave before the Reformation, but also applied to one found (as in Saxon times) on the outside of a church or on a standing cross.

ROUNDEL: A moulded opening or niche of circular form.

RUBBLE: Uncut stone of all shapes and sizes, laid at random without courses.

SCREEN: A generally elaborate barrier or division between portions of the church reserved for special

purposes, e.g. between nave and choir or chancel (see ROOD above), or between chantries or other chapels and nave, choir, chancel, transepts or aisles.

SEDILIA: Seats for priests, generally cut out of the south wall by the main altar.

SHAFT: Portion of a column between base and capital; also a small column supporting a vaulting rib.

SOFFIT: The ceiling, or underside, of any architectural member, e.g. of an arch.

SPANDREL: Space between the head of any arch (or door, window, etc.) and the frame in which it is set; also the space left between two adjoining arches.

SPLAY: Diagonal surface formed by the cutting away of the wall round a door or window; the opening then becomes wider inside than outside, or *vice versa*; hence 'splayed inwards' or 'outwards'.

SPRINGER: The lowest stone of an arch, rib or vault, at the point where the arch begins to 'spring'.

STRING-COURSE: A projecting band of stones, or moulding, along a wall.

TRACERY: Ornamental pattern(s) formed by the tracing, or interweaving, of the mullions in the head of a window; applied also to similar work in wood screens and panelling.

TRANSEPT: That part of a cruciform church which projects at right angles to the main building, usually to north and south, forming the arms of a cross; sometimes called a cross-aisle.

TRANSOM: Horizontal member of a window; the cross-bar.

TRIFORIUM: The middle space between the clerestory above, and the nave-piers and aisles below; it often forms a gallery or passage above the roofs of the aisles and, having no windows to the open air, is sometimes called a 'blind-story'.

TRUSS: A framed support for a roof, standing vertically, and dividing the roof into bays.

TYMPANUM: Semicircular or semioval slab, filling up the space between the lintel and arch of a door; generally (but not always) Saxon or Norman, since their doors were mainly set in rounded portals.

VAULT: An arched roof built with stone or brick.

VOUSSOIRS: Stones in an arch or vault, so trimmed that their sides taper towards the imaginary centre of the circle of that arch; thus the more pressure falls upon them, the more tightly they hold together.

Select bibliography

Origins of church buildings and the parish

Hugh Braun, *Parish Churches: their Architectural Development in England* (London, 1970). A.W. Clapham, *English Romanesque Architecture* (Oxford, 1930, 1934, especially vol. I), also *Romanesque Architecture in Western Europe* (Oxford, 1936). R.T. Stoll and J. Roubier, *Architecture and Sculpture in Early Britain* (London, 1967). J. Strzygowski, *Origins of Christian Church Art* (Oxford, 1923). D. Thomson, *Parish and Parish Church* (Baird Lecture, 1935, London, 1948).

General historical

M.D. Anderson (Lady Cox), *Looking for History in British Churches* (London, 1951). John Betjeman (ed.), *Collins Guide to English Parish Churches* (essays on English and Manx churches by various hands, with introduction and some county sections by Betjeman; London, 1958). Francis Bond, *An Introduction to English Church Architecture* (Oxford, 1913). Basil F.L. Clarke and John Betjeman, *English Churches* (London, 1964). G.H. Cook, *English Collegiate Churches* (London, 1959), and *The English Mediaeval Parish Church* (London, 1954, 1970). J. Charles Cox and Charles Bradley Ford, *The Parish Churches of England* (5th edn., ed. Ford; London, 1946–47). E. Tyrrell-Green, *Parish Church Architecture* (London, 1924).

Social and economic background

M.W. Beresford, *The Lost Villages of England* (London, 1954), and *New Towns of the Middle Ages* (London, 1967). W.G. Hoskins, *The Making of the English Landscape* (London, 1955, paperback 1970). S.L. Ollard and Gordon Cross, *A Dictionary of English Church History* (London, 1912, 1919). *The Oxford Dictionary of the Christian Church*, ed. F.L. Cross (2nd edn., rev. Cross and Livingstone, Oxford, 1974).

Styles, periods, regions

County by county the volumes of *The Victoria County History* and of the Royal Commission on Historical Monuments give architectural descriptions, diagrams, plans, etc. of churches in each county or sub-section thereof. Also *The Little Guides*, Batsford's 'County Church' guides (ed. J.C. Cox), Murray's *Guides* and the *Shell Guides* will be found useful.

F.J. Allen, *The Great Church Towers of England* (Cambridge, 1932). M.D. Anderson (Lady Cox), *Animal Carvings in British Churches* (Cambridge, 1938), *The Imagery of British Churches* (London, 1955),

and *The Medieval Carver; Misericords*. T.D. Atkinson, *Local Style in English Architecture* (London, 1947). Francis Bond, *The Chancel of English Churches* (1916), *Dedications and Patron Saints of English Churches* (1914), *English Church Architecture* (1913) contains descriptions of church details and elements, but see also his *Fonts and Font-covers* (Oxford, 1908), and *Screens and Galleries in English Churches* (1909). T. Borenius and E.W. Tristram, *English Medieval Painting* (1927). H. Miles Brown, *What to look for in Cornish Churches* (Newton Abbot, 1973). H. Munro Cautley, *Norfolk Churches* (London, 1973), and *Suffolk Churches* (London, 1973). C.J.P. Cave, *Roof Bosses in Medieval Churches* (Cambridge, 1948). Kenneth Clark, *The Gothic Revival* (London, 1964). Basil F.L. Clarke, *Church Builders of the Nineteenth Century* (1st edn. 1938), and *Parish Churches of London* (London, 1966). Alec Clifton-Taylor, *English Parish Churches as Works of Art* (London, 1974). J. Charles Cox, *Bench-ends in English Churches* (1916), *English Church Fittings, Furniture and Accessories* (London, 1923), and *Pulpits, Lecterns and Organs* (1915). F.H. Crossley, *English Church Monuments, AD 1150–1550* (London, 1921, 1933); with F.E. Howard, *English Church Woodwork* (London, 1918, 1933). Charles Eastlake, ed. J. Mordaunt Crook, *A History of the Gothic Revival* (Leicester, 1971). Katherine A. Esdaile, *English Church Monuments, 1510–1840* (London, 1946). E.A. Fisher, *Anglo-Saxon Towers* (Newton Abbot, 1969), *The Greater Anglo-Saxon Churches* (London, 1962), *An Introduction to Anglo-Saxon Architecture* (London, 1959), and *Saxon Churches of Sussex* (London, 1972). A.H. Gardner, *Alabaster Tombs* (Cambridge, 1940), and *English Medieval Sculpture* (Cambridge, 1951). Reinhard Gieselmann, *Contemporary Church Architecture* (London, 1972). George L. Hersey, *High Victorian Gothic* (London, 1972). Milburn, *Saints and their Emblems in English Churches* (Oxford, 1949). Nikolaus Pevsner, *Some Architectural Writers of the Nineteenth Century* (Oxford, 1972), and with others, *The Buildings of England Series* (London, various dates). Phoebe Stanton, *Pugin* (London, 1971). John Summerson, *Victorian Architecture* (New York, 1971). H.M. Taylor and Joan Taylor, *Anglo-Saxon Architecture* (Cambridge, 1965). E.W. Tristram and W.G. Constable, *English Medieval Wall Paintings, 12th Century* (1944). Aymer Vallance, *English Church Screens* (1936), and *Screens of Greater English Churches* (1947). Marcus Whiffen, *Stuart and Georgian Churches Outside London, 1603–1837* (London, 1947–48).

List of places, by counties

For page references, see the individual names in the index

Bedfordshire
Eaton Bray, Leighton Buzzard, Turvey, Woburn

Berkshire
Aldworth, Faringdon, North Hinksey, Reading, Uffington, Wantage

Bristol

Buckinghamshire
Dinton, Farnham Royal, Ivinghoe, Ludgershall, Quainton, Stewkley, Stone, Wendover, West Wycombe, Wing

Cambridgeshire
Bartlow, Cambridge, Ickleton, March, Westley Waterless

Cheshire
Astbury, Nantwich

Cornwall
Blisland, Goran, Launcells, Launceston, Madron, St Ives, St Winnow

Cumberland
Great Salkeld

Derbyshire
Ashbourne, Melbourne, Repton

Devon
Babbacombe, Bridford, Clyst St Lawrence, Cruwys Morchard, Cullompton, Exeter, Exmouth, Kenton, Molland, Ottery St Mary, Tiverton, Teignmouth, Torbryan

Dorset
Wareham, Whitechurch Canonicorum

Co. Durham
Durham, Escomb, Jarrow, Monkwearmouth, Roker Park

Essex
Abbess Roding, Blackmore, Bradwell juxta Mare, Castle Hedingham, Chrishall, Copford, Dedham, Great Bardfield, Great Canfield, Great Warley, Greenstead, Hempstead, Ingatestone, Lambourne, Layer Marney, Lindsell, Little Maplestead, Rochford, Saffron Walden, Sandon, Stebbing, Tilty, Wanstead

Gloucestershire
Ampney St Peter, Bagendon, Baunton, Bibury, the Cerneys, Chipping Campden, Cirencester, Daglingworth, Deerhurst, Didmarton, the Duntisbournes, Elkstone, Fairford, Gloucester, Kempley, Little Barrington, Moreton Valence, Northleach, Quenington, Stratton, Tetbury

Hampshire
Breamore, East Meon, New Romsey

Herefordshire
Abbey Dore, Castle Frome, Eardisley, Kilpeck, Ledbury, Leominster, Pembridge, Rowlstone, St Margaret's, Shobdon, Weobley

Hertfordshire
Anstey, Ashwell, Harpenden, St Albans, Walkern, Wheathampstead

Huntingdonshire
Leighton Bromswold, Little Gidding, Wittering, Yaxley

Kent
Barfreston, Borden, Canterbury, Chartham, Chiddingstone Causeway, Cliffe, Cranbrook, Lyminge, Mereworth, Patrixbourne, Reculver, Rochester, Staplehurst, Stone

Lancashire
Middleton, Wigan

Leicestershire
Bottesford, Breedon-on-the-Hill, Foxton, Kilworth, King's Norton, Market Bosworth, Quorndon, Ratby, Staunton Harold

Lincolnshire
Barton on Humber, Boston, Grantham, Great Ponton, Heckington, Kirkstead, Leverington, Lincoln, Long Sutton, Pickworth, Spalding, Stainby, Stamford, Stow, Sutterton, Threckingham, Wrangle

London

Middlesex
Harefield

Norfolk
Blakeney, Cley-next-the-Sea, East Dereham, Haddiscoe, Holkham, Ingham, Ludham, North Elmham, Norwich, Ranworth, Salle, South Lopham, Swaffham, Terrington St John, Tilney All Saints, Trunch, Walpole St Peter, Walsoken, West Walton

Northamptonshire
Barnack, Brixworth, Castor, Earls Barton, Finedon, Fotheringay, Geddington, Great Brington, Higham Ferrers, Northampton, Raunds, Stowe-Nine-Churches

Northumberland
Berwick on Tweed, Corbridge, Hexham, Lindisfarne, Newcastle-upon-Tyne

Nottinghamshire
Hawton, Lenton, Newark, Nottingham

247

Oxfordshire
Burford, Great Tew, Hanwell, Iffley, Langford, Oxford, Stanton Harcourt, Swinbrook, Witney

Rutland
Clipsham, Ketton, Lyddington, Tickencote, Tixover

Shropshire
Bromfield, Leebotwood, Ludlow, Onibury, Shifnal, Shrewsbury, Stanton Lacy, Tong

Somerset
Axbridge, Bath, Chew Magna, Chewton Mendip, Croscombe, Glastonbury, Huish Episcopi, Mells, Staple Fitzpaine, Taunton, Wells

Staffordshire
Burton on Trent, Hoar Cross, Ingestre, Weston, Wolverhampton

Suffolk
Acton, Bildeston, Blythburgh, Bramfield, Bungay, Dennington, Denston, East Bergholt, Eye, Fressingfield, Great Bealings, Icklingham, Ipswich, Kedington, Lavenham, Long Melford, Mildenhall, Monks Eleigh, Mutford, Needham Market, Southwold, Stoke by Nayland, Thornham Parva, Ufford, Westhall, Wickham Market, Woodbridge, Woolpit

Surrey
Chaldon, Croydon, Petersham, Stoke d'Abernon

Sussex
Ashburnham, Bishopstone, Brighton, Hastings, Rustington, Shoreham, Sompting, Worth

Warwickshire
Birley, Charlecote, Compton Wynyates, Over Whitacre, Stratford on Avon, Warwick

Wiltshire
Avebury, Bradford on Avon, Bromham, Cricklade, Edington, Hardenhuish, Inglesham, Lydiard Tregoze, Malmesbury, Salisbury

Worcestershire
Bredon, Chaddesley Corbett, Croome d'Abitot, Great Witley, Ombersley, Tardebigge, Worcester

Yorkshire
Adel, Beeford, Fountains, Halifax, Holme, Hull, Lastingham, Leeds, Patrington, Pickering, Skelton, Studley Royal, Thirsk, Tickhill, Wensley, Whitby, Woodthorpe, York

Index

252